GOOD DAMAGE

a memoir

Tragedy.

Lightly Polished,
with a Side of Optimism

TREY TOLER

Published by Ripples Media
Atlanta, Georgia
www.ripples.media

First printing 2026

Cover design concept by Andy Suggs
Full cover design by Ripples Media
Typesetting by Najdan Mancic

ISBN 978-1-971718-24-8 (Paperback)
ISBN 978-1-971718-25-5 (Hardcover)
ISBN 978-1-971718-23-1 (eBook)
Library of Congress Control Number: 2026907592

For my mom, everything good
in me came from you.

———————————

CONTENTS

NOT EVERYTHING
THAT BREAKS IS BAD

No spiritual glow-up. No reel called "How I Healed." No Bali retreat to find inner peace. No photo-ready stack of gratitude journals with perfectly centered handwriting.

And I'm not handing out ten life hacks to turn your pain into purpose before the next ad break.

I don't know your story.

But if even one line grazes into something familiar in you—that's enough.

Because I know what it feels like to smile through a normal-looking day while the inside of your life reeks like the mystery Tupperware you opened once, gagged, and burned sage over to release whatever demon had been fermenting inside.

The actual battle lies in the spaces we're not invited to—where we're left guessing who's drowning and who's just waving. When the problem is obvious, we don't hesitate:

Someone drops their groceries in the parking lot—eggs rolling, milk bleeding into the asphalt—you don't stop to analyze their childhood trauma, or life decisions.

You bend down. You grab the bag. You help.

That's instinct.

And maybe, as you walk away, there's a slight lift in your chest because you feel that discreet satisfaction of doing a good thing. Of showing up, just for a second, for someone else. You were *human*.

But what about the stuff that doesn't spill across the pavement? The parts pressed down so deep that not even the closest friends catch the strain. Those look more like everyday life.

We carry birthdays no one else remembers, and voicemails we can't listen to or delete.

We hold a dozen invisible burnout trophies, and instead of asking for help, we straighten our backs.

We whisper-Google "how to not screw up your kid" at 1:27 a.m., then spiral five minutes later, wondering if we've just triggered the makings of a Dateline episode—Keith Morrison warming up somewhere, ominous piano ready.

Then, eventually, we end up unloading the whole thing into ChatGPT, as if it were a priest in a confessional.

We don't call it unraveling.

We call it "getting shit done."

Smile wider.

It's wild how we treat emotional collapse like a performance review we're desperate to ace. And asking for help? That feels like handing in your resignation for trying to be "the one who has it together."

We still laugh—of course we do. But the laugh doesn't quite reach our eyes. Because behind the smile, there's a room no one else walks into, still burning.

Maybe that's you.

It's been me, too. And nobody came—not because they didn't care, but because I never let it show long enough to be caught.

Eventually, it all hits you—in the bathroom, under harsh fluorescent lights made by Satan: the fatigue, the tension, the creeping suspicion that your jaw has its own therapist now—from holding everything—*everything*—in place.

And we guard it with everything we have. Not because we're trying to be strong, or fake, or noble. But because somewhere along the way, we decided we weren't *allowed* to drop anything, to fall apart.

Until somewhere down the line, the mask stops being something to wear for everyone else. It becomes the only thing keeping our insides from leaking out. So we keep it on—even when it leaves us emotionally neutered.

I know that feeling; it's like muscle memory.

You do, too.

I was the guy people envied for "always having a smile." They saw the jokes, the energy, the charisma. What they didn't see was the kid sitting beside his mother's oxygen machine, watching her sort through bills she had no way

to cover—then walking into school the next morning like nothing was wrong.

That kind of split lives in your DNA.

And if I'm being honest, we all pick up more than we ever say out loud.

We don't always step in, but we notice.

And that's the tell, isn't it?—the small, unmistakable sign that we're still wired to care.

Not being a fixer—trust me, I put in my hours.

Early on, I honestly believed that if I said the *right thing* to someone who was hurting or hit them with the perfect piece of perspective, they'd snap back to themselves. But, it turns out people aren't vending machines. You can't insert wisdom and expect healing to tumble out the bottom.

There's something sacred in just *being there*, without offering a five-step plan or some perfectly timed motivational quote. Sitting with someone in the middle of their mess without trying to clean it up for them, the way someone once did for me. Just being a presence they can lean toward without having to explain every detail.

And sometimes it isn't a heart-to-heart. It's rewatching *Schitt's Creek* together with a glass of wine and barely speaking, or taking a hike where conversation flows in and out—half jokes, half memories. Nothing reaches some significant conclusion, yet somehow everything that matters gets said anyway.

That's what I want this book to be. Not a fix. Not a plan. Just something you can return to—when your mask starts pressing in, and you're tired of pretending it still fits.

When we share slices of our life—messy, traumatic, unfinished—we make it easier for someone else to breathe. You never know what opens up when judgment steps aside, and honesty takes the seat it should have had all along.

It might be what keeps someone here when staying feels impossible.

I haven't figured it all out. Not even close. But I've tripped through enough darkness to know this: you don't have to do it alone. And maybe not everything that breaks is a loss.

Some damage?

That's where the good stuff starts to grow.

A place where something honest pushes through and takes hold.

The *Good Damage*.

THE VERSION
THEY LOVED

The mic's live and the crowd's quiet. You glance around for cues, watching how the confident ones move and pray your voice doesn't crack when it's your turn. Everyone else seems to hit their cues perfectly, like they've been rehearsing for years. Meanwhile, you're hoping you don't trip over a chair or on your own thoughts.

If that resonates with you, we're in the same scene.

Somewhere between recess and roll call, you start to understand the rules no one bothers to explain. Not the written ones, the other set. The ones kids absorb without realizing they're learning anything at all.

The loud kids were the first to be corrected: a teacher's raised brow, a pointed pause, the subtle cue to dial themselves down. The quiet ones weren't spared either—pulled aside

after class and encouraged to "find their voice," as if belonging required turning the volume up past their comfort.

Then there were the kids who learned in their own method, who stared out the window to think, who tapped their pencil when the room felt too still, who needed the answer to make sense before they could speak it. They were marked as distractions, even when all they were doing was trying to stay afloat.

And the kids who colored past the borders on purpose — because the little square they were given didn't look anything like them. They weren't defiant. They were searching for a place on the page that felt honest.

Every one of them heard the same message:

There's a right way to exist here. Yours isn't it.

Conditioning begins here, not from lectures or punishments, but from tiny cues you catch in the corners of people's expressions—the shrugged-off corrections. The sighs adults release when they think you're not paying attention. Little by little, you learn exactly what parts of you the world meets with open arms—and what you're expected to keep behind the curtain.

Suddenly, we're trimming ourselves to fit the room. Not a full reinvention—just minor adjustments. Softer laugh. Straighter posture. A smile rehearsed in the bathroom mirror, adjusting the head tilt until it looks natural. We study our reflections like they're pop quizzes. Lift the chin. Loosen the shoulders. Add a hint of charm. A performance, but subtle enough that no one calls it one.

Some kids chase gold stars until their stomachs knot

from pressure. Others figure out how to disappear, drifting through hallways unnoticed, hoping invisibility counts as safety. And then there are the ones who compensate by dialing everything up—stories bigger, laughter louder, personality turned into armor.

Eventually, our roles settle in.

The honor student.

The comic relief.

The athlete.

Different masks, same goal.

Each of us presenting the version we learned would draw the least resistance and the most affection.

By the time we reach adulthood, we've logged years of dress rehearsals—perfecting how to answer "How are you?" without accidentally telling the truth. Life becomes a patchwork of roles—versions of ourselves we built to survive. Eventually, you speak the language of expectations so fluently you barely notice you're translating yourself in real time.

And then one day, you catch your reflection mid-routine and realize you're watching a performance you've been running for so long, you're almost convinced it was the real thing.

In kindergarten, discipline came in the form of craft supplies. A plastic bucket sat on the teacher's desk, filled with bright felt worms, each one the size of a finger, and smugly cheerful. If you talked out of turn, she'd nod toward the bucket, and you'd make the slow walk to grab one. Then came the real punishment: sticking it onto the paper apple with your name written in wide, wobbly letters. The apple hung on the wall for everyone to study during snack time and story hour.

That day, during a lesson, I got caught mid-conversation—again. The teacher didn't even look up, just pointed to the bucket. On my walk of shame, I picked out the brightest worm, held it between my fingers, and whispered, "Sorry, little buddy," before pressing it onto my apple.

A tiny moment of empathy, talking to a worm, was the last straw. The teacher sighed, the other kids laughed, and I was escorted straight to the hallway. By the end of some days, my apple looked less like a fruit and more like a warning label.

I wasn't trying to be disruptive—I just loved getting a laugh. It was like oxygen. I had too many thoughts and exactly one mouth. ADHD made sure every idea felt like an emergency, every emotion showed up in all caps, bolded, and screaming *NOW.*

That worm moment is Exhibit A in my Myers-Briggs personality profile, ENFJ. I'm constantly narrating, always connecting. Emotionally fluent. Think: Google Translate for feelings nobody asked me to interpret. I've always had the volume of a hype man and the heart of a therapist.

I've talked to people, animals, inanimate objects—anything that might be carrying emotion, even if I had to imagine it. I didn't know how to turn off connection mode. Still don't. If something has a face, I'm already in a relationship with it.

Which might explain the leash.

My mom actually had me on a leash when I was young. Beige. Velcro. Strapped to my wrist: a toddler parole bracelet. I had a three-foot radius and zero chill—working that space like I was headlining Coachella for the feral and emotionally unregulated.

Nothing in my radius was off limits. Shopping with my mom, mannequins became my stage partners. I'd yank their skirts down—quick costume changes in a one-man show nobody asked for, but I was absolutely nailing.

Since I couldn't run, I orbited. I wound myself around store displays like I was setting traps, maneuvering myself into their corners until my mom had to peel me out. My favorite hideout was the circular clothing rack—polyester jungle on the outside, secret world within. I'd dive in and vanish, then crawl out growling at strangers like some strip mall-dwelling cryptid on the loose.

I literally never stopped.

Only got leash-dragged out of the store once—at least that I remember—no clue what triggered it. Maybe my mom spent too long flipping through clearance racks. Maybe the store's playlist offended my spirit; there's only so much "Blame It on the Rain" by Milli Vanilli a person can take before they snap.

All I know is I locked eyes with a circular rack of blouses and took off as if it dared me not to. I grabbed hold like it was a carnival ride—legs pumping, face committed—training for NASA with the conviction Katy Perry brought to her eleven-minute Space Uber flight.

Seconds later, I was airborne. I hit the tile in a tangle of polyester and poor decisions. The aftermath looked part hurricane, part women's casuals-based exorcism.

Gasps erupted. Handbags were clutched.

The final hanger hit the tile with the force of a courtroom drama—clang! Guilty. On all counts.

And me? I cracked up. No remorse. Full-volume chaos giggle.

It wasn't a choice. I didn't workshop my material. I just entered the world already mid-bit. My humor showed up first, before anything else. People liked that version of me. And honestly? So did I. It was shinier and less complicated than the other parts spinning beneath it.

Your version might look different.

Maybe your mask comes stamped with achievement—organized, efficient, always one step ahead. The dependable one people call when something goes sideways. Or perhaps you built an identity around self-sufficiency, which looks strong from a distance but is really just fear wearing a costume of confidence.

Others slip into roles that keep peace, reading the mood of a room before they even cross the threshold, adjusting themselves to match whoever needs them most—the one most likely to earn an easy smile—the version least likely to unsettle anyone.

We master the art of moderation, sharing a spark of personality bright enough to seem genuine but never bright enough to draw the wrong kind of attention.

It becomes second nature, offering just the right amount of ourselves to keep the room at ease.

So you keep performing it.

Because that's the version they loved.

NO WORRIES AT ALL :)

We post the polished version, filter at 70%, caption at peak relatability, hoping the market buys it. Maybe if the algorithm approves, we can too.

Then we refresh.

We talk a big game about not caring about likes—"I'm above all that." And then, five seconds after posting, we slam the "hide like count" option before there's a chance to expose what we fear most: that the only applause in the room is coming from us. Hyping ourselves in a digital broom closet nobody else wandered into.

And still, we insist we're thriving. Career soaring. Side projects are flourishing. Emotional baggage tucked away in some mental storage unit labeled *circle back when life slows down,* which, of course, it never does.

We keep the performance polished because it's easier than admitting that the backstage looks nothing like the show.

And still, we're out here texting out messages like:

No worries at all :)

LOL, just busy!

Polite, upbeat, and nowhere near the truth.

Social media doesn't just keep the masks in place; it buffs them to a shine. Scroll long enough, and it feels less like life and more like a gallery exhibit: sunsets without a single car in sight, babies who apparently came out of the womb sleep-trained, and couples who only argue over who's more in love with whom.

And then there's the productivity prophet on LinkedIn, the guy in the tight black tech bro tee who swears the secret to success is waking up at 3 a.m. to chug raw eggs, journal his quarterly intentions, pulverize kale into something "disruptive," and rake that tiny sand garden next to his monitor. Hence, his workflow remains "aligned with purpose." He explains it in a 37-part carousel post, of course.

And even when we *know* it's curated—when we can practically see the filters and the retakes baked into every square, we still catch ourselves stacking our real life against someone else's highlight reel, wondering why our reality feels so different.

If it required thirty attempts, a glowing ring light, and a caption solely optimized for engagement, that's not life.

That's marketing.

The first time I truly grasped the burden of perfection was the day I slipped on a brand-new pair of sneakers and instantly

regretted having feet. They were blinding, so bright they could have guided an aircraft. The kind of sneakers that dared the world to come near them but also shrieked in terror at the idea of touching an actual surface.

I perched on the edge of my bed, tugging gently at the laces with the reverence of someone handling museum artifacts. Every loop felt precious. Every pull felt dangerous. One scuff and the whole illusion would crumble.

And then came the fear.

I refused to bend them. That first crease across the toe box felt catastrophic, the moment your sneakers dropped from "fresh out the box" to "regular shoes," all because you dared to walk. So I avoided it with every ounce of determination a kid can muster. I shuffled down the hallway flat-footed, moving in stiff, careful steps—a full Frankenstein glide. I looked less like a child heading to class and more like someone portraying an enchanted tree in a school play who took method acting too far.

No adult warned me about this. There was no official briefing, no all-school announcement about crease prevention. No seasoned sneakerhead appeared in a dim Foot Locker stockroom to pass down sacred instructions.

I just...knew.

Some inner committee convened without my consent, and the verdict came back clear:

New must remain unmarked.

Clean must avoid contamination.

Anything less felt ruined. There was no "good enough," no room for scuffs or life happening. It was either pristine or pointless.

Until eventually, it happened. The leather folded, the crease showed up, and I absolutely lost it. One bend and I short-circuited. You'd think I'd accidentally set fire to a national monument. I was six, staring at my shoes like they came with an "always looks new" warranty—and I'd just voided it.

And honestly? I still do it.

Not with shoes (fine, yes, still with shoes—thank you, OCD). But with everything else, too. With people. With feelings. With myself.

I catch the same instinct—tiptoeing mentally, careful not to mark anything. Adjusting, monitoring, overthinking, and trying to stay uncreased. Almost like: if the surface stays spotless, the rest of me might too. Like being pristine on the outside might fool someone into thinking the inside is just as sorted.

Most people see the version of you that's been focus-grouped for public consumption. The one that's been scrubbed, soft-launched, and market-tested for likability. We're told to be authentic, but only within the parameters of what won't make anyone shift in their seat. Share your growth, yes—but skip the part where the growth came from being knocked down flat. So you zip the more challenging emotions into something compact and carry them through the day like they're travel-sized.

We're all basically running our own tiny PR agencies, managing our image one invisible press release at a time. Highlighting the traits we hope people latch onto—it's almost universal: different lives, same instinct.

The settings change, but the ache doesn't. Whether it's money, status, a bigger house, or a corner office—it all buys comfort, not peace. None of it reaches the places that actually hurt. You can renovate your living room all you want, but you can't redecorate your way out of something that needs healing from the inside out.

There's only so long you can force a smile before your face starts to cramp. And when the curtain finally slips—when you see that people weren't attached to *you,* but to the image you've curated, it hits with a strange kind of grief.

Walking around with creases isn't failure; it's proof you're moving. Proof you've stepped into the world instead of tiptoeing around it. Scuffs come from effort. From showing up. From choosing to participate in your own life instead of preserving yourself in some pristine, untouched state.

BEFORE/AFTER

In third grade, I fell into an easy friendship with a kid named Kyle.

We got paired for a class project and spent an entire week hunched over a shoebox diorama, debating over where the volcano should go and why a T. rex absolutely belonged in a prehistoric swamp scene that made no room for him. Kyle insisted it didn't fit. I insisted it made the whole thing worth looking at.

The first afternoon I went to his house, I stepped into a world that felt impossibly warm. We spread our supplies across the kitchen table. Kyle focused on the assignment. I kept glancing around, taking in the little things: a row of photos on the fridge, a stack of mail that hadn't toppled over, a bowl of fruit that looked untouched because someone always replaced it.

At Kyle's house, before you even set your fork down, someone was already asking you if you wanted more—no hesitation, no performative politeness. It was instinct for them.

His parents had this way of smiling that didn't stop at their mouths. It lifted through their whole expression, settling into their eyes and even the way they held themselves. You felt noticed there, accounted for without having to earn it.

Kyle carried around a baseball glove that had survived more summers than a third grader should reasonably remember. The leather was beaten to hell from use, the laces barely keeping it together, but he treated it like treasure. He kept it with him everywhere, stuffed in his backpack, wedged under his arm as he walked to the bus, propped on the desk during class as if a recess miracle might break out. That glove was his ticket to someplace bigger, even if he couldn't name where.

We ended up in the same class again in fifth grade. Then sixth. By then, our friendship felt baked into the school year—another subject on the schedule.

The summer before seventh grade moved slowly, the kind of days that left you peeling yourself off the furniture by midday. About a month before school started, Kyle and his dad were driving back from somewhere, most likely practice, most likely mid-debate about batting averages, Kyle's glove riding shotgun like a third passenger.

A dump truck ran a stop sign.

That was the whole story. No warning. One moment, they were heading home, and the next, the road folded their lives in on itself. Kyle didn't make it to the hospital.

He didn't make it to seventh grade.

There was no strange feeling beforehand, nothing that made the day stand out in memory. It was a regular Wednesday until it wasn't, and the world didn't pause to acknowledge the difference. It just kept going.

I've thought about Kyle and his family ever since. Not every day, but often enough for his absence to tap me on the shoulder at random. We grow up assuming we'll sense the approach of a turning point, that something will cue us in.

But real life doesn't tease that's coming. It moves forward without a hint, and you catch up when you can.

Certain moments redraw the map of your life in one stroke: the version you lived in before you knew, and the one left after that you couldn't forget.

One minute, you're a person who's never lost a job.

Never had your heart handed back to you.

Never answered a call that rearranged your entire bloodstream.

Then life does what life does.

The phone rings.

A door slams hard enough to tell you everything you need to know without saying a word.

A slip of paper lands in your hands, and suddenly, HR is using phrases like "restructuring."

A doctor steps back from the screen with a breath that doesn't belong in a routine checkup.

And in that instant, the version of you who existed five minutes earlier is gone, no farewell tour, no ceremony, not even a decent exit interview—just gone.

You don't realize you were living in the Before until you've already crossed into the After, standing there with that stunned look people get when they're trying to understand the new terms of their own existence. Trying to absorb that nothing will return to what it was.

So this is permanent.

Now what?

We walk around assuming we have endless renewals—as if life were some annual subscription that automatically renews.

But all it takes is one moment, one sentence, one random event in the day, and you become someone you've never met.

Someone without an option to turn around.

Joy and grief aren't opposites. They're awkward roommates that life assigns without warning.

Joy leaves dishes in the sink. Grief labels their leftovers and slams doors at 3 a.m. But somehow, they both live here now—and neither's breaking the lease.

We make the mistake of thinking that we have to choose one. We believe joy means we're healed. That grief means we're broken.

We recognize joy only because loss marked us first. We recognize grief *because* we've loved something so deeply that it hurts when it's gone. Both emotions trace the same outline: You risked. You felt. You let something matter enough to change you.

If today were the last time you saw the people you love, would any of the nonsense taking up real estate in your mind even stand a chance?

The spiraling.

The career you've welded to your identity.

The calorie arithmetic you pretend is "wellness."

The almost-relationships you water just enough to keep alive, secretly hoping they will die so you don't have to initiate a breakup with someone you were never *actually* dating.

Then there's the approval you chase from people who wouldn't bother showing up to your memorial.

The way you punish yourself for missing some made-up milestone, convinced it disqualifies you from being a functional human.

The compulsive checking—messages, emails, views—as if your worth is hiding in a notification badge.

We spend so much of our lives trying to out-perfect life so we don't have to *feel* it, that you don't even notice how much of your life you're trading just to feel safe.

Would any of it matter if today were the last day your body ever moved this easily? Would any of it *still* deserve that kind of devotion?

We tell ourselves there's plenty of time, that we'll show up the next round, without pausing to notice how many chances we let slip.

But there is no next time, only *this* once.

This breath you barely notice as it leaves you.

This version of you that still believes today will end the same way it began.

This you, still whole, untouched by the moment already heading your way.

THE MONSTERS WE LEARN TO NAME

Before I had a name for it, it showed up in my posture. It lived in the way I trained my voice to sit differently in my throat. I wasn't like the other boys—I sensed that long before anyone felt the need to say it. The way my voice, though loud enough to fill any room, carried a softness that didn't quite belong to boys.

And trust me, they did say it. Sometimes loudly.

I didn't need anyone to tell me. I heard it in the way they laughed, the way they tilted their heads and said, "Why do you sound like that?" as if my existence needed an explanation.

In second grade, I stood in the kickball line, hands folded neatly in front of me, rocking side to side. A boy behind me muttered something under his breath. I missed the words, but when I turned around, his smirk said enough. I dropped my hands fast, shoved them into my pockets—like that could bury whatever part of me he'd spotted.

At home, I rehearsed how to exist. Shoulders pulled back. Feet planted just right. Hands swinging easily, as if I didn't need to think about where to put them. The mirror was relentless. It caught everything—the sway in my hips, the way my elbows floated when I spoke. A thousand tiny tells. None loud enough to name, all loud enough to feel. No matter how carefully I arranged myself, something always slipped through—something I couldn't un-train.

I watched my friends move through the world with the ease of people who never had to second-guess their place in it. They laughed without scanning the room first, slouched in chairs as if comfort was their birthright. Just being themselves looked effortless—like breathing.

I studied that ease the way some people study scripture, searching for a line that might save me. I envied it, and if I'm honest, I resented it too. While they ran wild, I learned to move carefully, to measure my tone, my hands, my presence.

In classrooms, at lunch tables, on their living room floors, I sat among them and wondered what it felt like to live without rehearsal—to let a word leave my mouth without first checking its pitch, to speak before running lines in your head. That kind of freedom felt untouchable, a privilege reserved for kids who didn't have to hide pieces of themselves just to make it through the day.

I thought I'd mastered the art of blending in. But the playground always called my bluff. Boys slammed into each

other, all knees and elbows and noise, and I lingered at the edge—close enough to watch, far enough to stay untouched.

"Why don't you ever join in?" someone asked me once, their tone more accusatory than curious. I mumbled something about not liking to get dirty, but the truth was, I didn't know how to join. It was like watching a foreign film with no subtitles—except the plot was dodgeball and the stakes were my dignity.

There were moments I almost forgot about the secret, when its shadow fell behind me instead of on top of me. But it never stayed gone for long. "Why do you walk like that?" or "Why do you sound like that?" It was always *that*, ambiguous and yet so painfully clear.

I'd laugh, play it off, and hand them a joke before I could become one. The jokes always worked; it made them comfortable again—but more importantly, it made them forget. But I never did. Their questions stayed with me long after everyone else moved on. They replayed in my head like a song I couldn't turn off. *Why do I walk like this? Why am I like this?*

It wasn't just the other kids. Adults noticed it, too, though their comments were more subtle. "You're sensitive—there's nothing wrong with that," muttered in a tone that suggested there was, in fact, something wrong with that. I learned to read between the lines before I could sound out the words on a page. I didn't need to understand sentences or context; they were written all over their faces.

Sports weren't my world. I wasn't the kid bolting out the door with a football tucked under my arm, chasing the sound

of cheers. Maybe it was a lack of exposure. Or perhaps it was something more profound—an instinct to sidestep the spaces where fathers and sons were supposed to bond. Spaces that only seemed to turn up the volume on the silence between my dad and me.

I don't remember my parents ever being married. It was always my mom, my sister, and me, our small triangle that worked because it had to. By the time I was four, they'd separated, and my memories of my dad are scattered, short clips instead of whole scenes. He carried an energy that didn't fit inside our house; even the walls seemed to tense when he walked in the door.

I can still feel the ball in my hands—too big, too slick, like it belonged to someone else. He'd throw it with an easy confidence that made me tense up before the ball even left his hand. It was like he belonged in that moment, and I was just visiting.

"Keep your eye on the ball, Trey!" The snap of his voice caught me off guard, intentional and sudden like a trigger pulled mid-sentence. I flinched as if something inside of me were yanked taut.

I tried. God, did I try.

I locked onto the ball until my eyes burned, every muscle straining like I could will it into my hands. I wasn't chasing the catch; I was chasing the look on his face when I finally got it right. Maybe, if I were the kind of son he wanted, he'd find a reason to come back.

The ball arced gracefully toward me, a perfect spiral. For a split second, I thought *maybe this time*. But it slipped

through my fingers again, landing with a hollow thud in the grass.

"Why are you ducking? CATCH THE BALL!" His voice cracked through the backyard, ricocheting off the fence like a warning shot. My arms flew up in reflex, flailing like one of those sad inflatable tube men with a slow leak.

"I'm scared it will hit my face," I muttered, the words barely audible—somewhere between shame and a plea for understanding. My eyes stayed fixed on the grass, tracing the patchy grass beneath my feet. I didn't even need to look up to feel it—his frustration radiated off the ground.

He laughed, sarcastic and joyless, "That's what happens in sports, Trey. You get hit. You bleed. You'll sometimes get a black eye."

His choice of words was blunt and settling—like a verdict. I wanted to explain that it wasn't the ball, not really. It was him. His tone, the way his patience thinned around me, did more damage than a fastball ever could. But I said nothing. Swallowed hard. Blinked fast and blamed the sun for the sting, anything but admit the truth: it was how he looked at me—like I'd already come up short.

"Focus!" he barked.

But I wasn't watching the ball. I was trying to crack the ever-evolving rulebook of masculinity—his version, anyway.

Sunscreen? Gay.

Flip flops? Gay.

Umbrellas? Apparently, for women and British tourists.

A man's hand on another man's shoulder? Immediate Vatican alert—we're one gesture away from a full-blown exorcism.

He didn't rant or rage—his disdain didn't come in explosions.

It came in casual drops of *wisdom*—comments tossed out with total conviction: "Real men don't ask for directions." "Real men know how to change their own oil."

These weren't lessons passed down with care; they were landmines, casually strewn across my childhood and waiting for me to take one wrong step. It felt like I was living inside a parody of masculinity, where sacred text ends up on the back of a Bass Pro Shops receipt.

Tiptoeing felt too dainty, or stomping would be too obvious—so I walked straight through the killing fields, trying to look confident while bracing for the next explosion.

And I always seemed to step wrong.

"Catching isn't hard," he said, shaking his head like I was an equation he inexplicably couldn't solve.

But it *was* hard.

Not because of the ball, but because of what it represented. But it was never about catching. It was an evaluation, an undisclosed audition for what he thought a son should be. You know, things that all boys should inherently be good at. Every throw was a question I couldn't answer, and every miss felt like proof he already knew that.

No matter how many balls I finally caught, no matter how hard I tried to play the part, I'd always miss the target he had in mind.

The South wasn't for boys like me. We lived deep in the backs of closets, tucked behind winter coats no one wore—present, but out of sight. Here, visibility felt dangerous. You

could wear color, just not *too* much of it. And God forbid you cross your legs the wrong direction or show up knowing the difference between cream and ivory. That alone could trigger an emergency prayer circle.

I am a Christian. I've always believed in God; that part was steady.

It was confusing, holding that belief while sitting in a church pew, feeling like I was both worshiper and defendant. The judgment had already taken up residence in me, calmly unpacking somewhere between "Amazing Grace" and the offering plate.

People meant well when they said things like, "One day when you meet a nice Christian woman..." and I'd nod like, *totally*, while picturing us color-coordinating casseroles for the church potluck. She'd be lovely—sweet, kind, someone I'd absolutely trust with my secrets and skincare routine, but not my wife.

And it's not like I was imagining myself riding off into the sunset with a man, either—not at that age. It just didn't compute. I didn't have the vocabulary for what it was; I just knew *that* story wasn't mine. Even as a kid, I could feel it, that mismatch between who I was and who I was supposed to be.

I couldn't tell you the scripture, the sermon title, or what color tie the pastor had on, but I remember the moment his voice hit *that* word, *homosexual*. He said it carefully, like it was contagious—something you might catch if you stood too close. Something that could happen if you weren't *right* with your Lord and Savior, Jesus Christ.

"Abomination," the pastor would say, slowly and

deliberately. "A-bom-i-na-tion," his head tilting just enough to let the word breathe. "Being gay," he would say, "was a lifestyle choice—a temptation you entertained—then gave into."

Those words made me feel like a defect in the system. Something to be handled, managed, and prayed over until it went away. Leviticus 18:22, it always dropped in like the biblical version of a pop-up ad you couldn't close. I almost expected the choir to back him up, repeating it like the chorus of a song.

I just sat there, my heart pounding hard enough to drown out the rest of the sermon. *Can they see it in me? Can they tell? Were they looking at me when he said, "homosexual"?*

I hadn't spoken. I hadn't really moved. But somehow I was convinced the entire sanctuary could read my mind—and that it had traces of glitter on it.

My hands locked so tightly until my fingers trembled, and I prayed harder than anyone in that room. Around me, rows of bowed heads swayed in unison, but I wasn't praying like them. I was bargaining. "Please, God," I begged, my lips barely moving. "Take this away. I'll do anything. Just don't let me be like *this*."

I never felt "Christian enough." At seven, my concept of theology was simple: Jesus died for our sins, so we should probably make Him proud.

I'm pretty sure Jesus wouldn't have been thrilled with my *Saved by the Bell* daydreams—that I wanted to be more than friends with Zack Morris and A.C. Slater. Zack had that smirk that made you want to forgive him for everything, and Slater's dimples deserved their own spin-off.

I didn't know what any of it meant, only that my crushes wore sneakers, had perfect hair, and stirred feelings that probably wouldn't fly at Vacation Bible School. The "sexuality" part came later. As a kid, I only knew my attention wasn't where it was supposed to be.

Being Christian, I carried the constant ache that I was letting God down. Sitting in those wooden pews, I'd lift my head before the prayer was finished and look up at the stained glass and feel like every color was brighter than what I deserved.

I felt a shame that made me wonder if heaven came with fine print, grace for everyone, *terms and conditions apply.* Because if what they said was true, how could there be a place up there for someone like me? For an abomination.

As a kid, an *abomination* sounded like something that lived under beds and inside closets. The type of thing you prayed away before the lights went out. I pictured myself as that thing, half-boy, half-sin, hoping God would forget I existed long enough for me to sneak past the gates.

And sometimes I'd lie awake and wonder, *do they even let monsters into heaven?*

WOMAN DOWN

While I was praying away the monster inside me, another had already taken up residence in our house. This one didn't care about secrets or shame. It didn't care who saw it.

It settled in my mother's lungs like it signed a lease. And that's how the next decade began in 1995, the year our lives exhaled and never quite caught their breath again.

My mother's beauty stood on its own. Wide, steady, hazel eyes, they saw everything but didn't give anything away. In one of my favorite pictures, she looked like a still from a 1970s film—one of those moments where the actress doesn't speak, but the camera lingers anyway, because it knows there's more going on beneath the surface.

She's standing in front of a wall of framed art. Her hair falls in a perfect, dark curtain, parted down the middle, not

a strand out of place. Her skin carries that deep sun-soaked bronze you only get from spending real time in the sun—hours stretched out under the heat of Atlanta summers, no sunscreen, only oil.

Her dress is sleeveless, yellow, tailored to her frame, with a bold white stripe running across the front at an angle. And then there's her smile. Slight but certain. It's the look of someone completely at ease in her own skin, like the world bent a little to make room for her shine.

Sometimes I look at that picture and wonder if she had any idea what was coming.

The nineties came in swinging, dragging one of the hardest decades of my mother's life behind them. By the end of '89, my parents had separated; by the following year, the divorce papers were signed—final ink on a story that had already ended long before.

For the first time in over a decade, my mom went back to work. The world she left had sped up. Typewriters replaced by keyboards, memos by emails, and letters by fax machines. Everything looked familiar, but much faster and less forgiving.

When fall came around, it brought more loss. Her mother died suddenly, a brain aneurysm ruptured. My sister was starting her senior year of high school, and I was walking into kindergarten with a backpack too big for my shoulders.

Before my mom landed her full-time job with the state, before the title, the desk, and the morning traffic she'd come to curse—she did whatever it took to keep us afloat. She picked up temp work and odd jobs, piecing together paychecks like puzzle pieces. One of them was delivering phone books, back when those still meant something. She'd load the trunk until it sagged, windows down, square her shoulders, and hit the road—faith in the passenger seat and pure grit behind the wheel.

There was also this little gas station down the street from our house called *Grands*.

I remember a few times we didn't stop for gas. Instead, my mom would pull into a corner spot, far left side of the lot, engine ticking as it cooled.

"Come on," she said. I followed.

Grands smelled like fried chicken biscuits, burnt coffee, and cigarettes. She carried her purse under one arm like it was part of her body, smiled at the cashier, then led me down to the end of the first aisle—to the bathroom.

"Stand over here, Trey." And she locked the door. She moved fast. One hand on her purse, the other reaching for the extra roll stacked on the back of the toilet tank. I watched her slide it into her bag like she was putting away lipstick. Zipped it shut.

No explanation. Just survival—executed clean and with enough composure that five-year-old me thought maybe this was just something adults did sometimes.

She never said we couldn't afford it. Never made it dramatic. We got back in the car. She turned up the radio. And that was that.

After that, my mom hustled so we'd never be in that spot again.

Every morning, long before the sun reached Marietta, suburb of Atlanta, my mom was already on the road after she'd drop me off at daycare. She worked inside one of those nondescript office buildings off Northside Drive. The car told her story better than any diary could, console tattooed with cup rings, the backseat a collage of crumpled worksheets and half-eaten snacks.

Every alarm, every stoplight, every crawl through traffic on that eighteen-mile stretch into Atlanta was part of that promise she never broke. By the time she reached the end of our driveway, our house sat right off a five-lane road, the morning rush stacked bumper-to-bumper. The world was already in motion before she'd even had a chance to breathe. Her life ran the same way, no gaps, no pause, just one long stretch of movement.

We were running late for daycare again. Mom's voice had that edge that said she'd already used up half her patience for the day, somewhere between wrangling me into the car and the traffic light that wouldn't turn green. "Trey, as soon as we get there, I need you to hop out, okay?"

Five-year-old logic: *be ready to launch.*

"Look, Mom! I already put my backpack on!" I announced, beaming as I'd just solved world hunger. "This way I won't forget it in the car. Now I can just hop out!"

The place was already pure chaos, with kids crying, minivans stacked three-deep. She whipped into the KinderCare parking lot, barely tapping the brakes, and before the tires even stopped rolling, I threw the door open like I was in a stunt movie. My seatbelt was still half-on, my backpack snagged on the buckle and snapped me sideways, and suddenly I was horizontal, backpack dragging across the asphalt.

Mom slammed the car in park, ran around the door, screaming my name. I was fine—more than fine. I thought it was hilarious. She was in tears; I was howling with laughter.

"Why would you do something like that?" she cried, eyes wide, voice pivoting between fear and fury.

I remember blinking at her, completely serious. "You told me to hop out when we got here."

After work, she crawled through the same gridlocked stretch of road that'd already mocked her patience just hours before. She'd pull into the carport and sit there for a moment, engine ticking, probably saying a silent prayer that I hadn't brought home another pink slip from school.

Then the door flew open, and her third shift started: Mom.

Keys clamped between her teeth, purse sliding down her arm, grocery bags biting into her wrists. The plastic stretched to its limit, because God forbid she make two trips.

"Hey, Trey!" she'd call out in that warm, syrupy Southern drawl that somehow made everything sound like good news. I'd already be laughing, because I knew what came next. Without fail, she'd drop her keys, kick off her shoes, and announce she had to pee, like it was a surprise every single day.

My mom downed water like a marathoner but had the bladder of a toddler, which meant the moment she got home, it was a race against time. I called it her "bathroom dance." Groceries hit the counter, purse slid off her arm, and she'd do this frantic shuffle down the hallway, laughing the whole way to the bathroom.

I thought my mom was invincible; part woman, part superhero. She could stir a pot of spaghetti with one hand,

while wrangling my chaos with the other, the oven clicking behind her as toast charred and our dog barked at whatever ghosts he thought he saw in the yard. She kept everything moving. Everything together.

But at night, I'd hear it. You couldn't miss the steady grind of her teeth. It was everything she carried and never said out loud—her stress, her anger, the sadness she didn't have time to process. Even in her sleep, she couldn't let go.

Every superhero has a weakness. I didn't know my mom's until 1995, when it started with something small, a cough. At first, it was forgettable, innocuous—just clear your throat to shake off. Only it never left.

At first, she brushed it aside. She always had things to do, people to take care of, and a family to hold together. But that cough was the first fracture in her invincibility, the tiny sound that started to undo the fairytale I'd built around her.

A week after the cough started, something in her pace changed. Mom moved more slowly; her steps became deliberate, as if she were wading through some unseen force.

"I'm fine," she said, voice hoarse and small, as if she could outrun the worry on my face by saying it fast enough. Then came the sound. Less a cough, more a machine misfiring with all the grace of an engine choking on its last attempt to start.

She reached for the kitchen counter, her fingers tightening around the edge until her knuckles went pale. The effort it took to steady herself said more than she'd ever admit. A few weeks earlier, she'd powered through a round of antibiotics—the strong kind, the kind that was supposed to wipe everything out. Clearly, it hadn't.

I was nine, too young to grasp what was happening, but old enough to recognize that something had changed. My mom wasn't okay, no matter how many times she said she was. The woman who used to move through life as if nothing could touch her had only the strength that flickered in small, simple ways.

The doctor admitted mom to the hospital, and our house—once predictable, once her domain—felt like someone had rearranged it in the dark. That was the beginning, the moment my mom's life started syncing to the rhythm of hospital monitors and intake forms. Every year that followed, '96, '97, '98, and on, seemed to orbit those fluorescent-lit rooms. Hospitals became the backdrop of my adolescence.

It's also when I learned to track her health the way sailors watch the horizon, reading signs no one else noticed. You didn't need a forecast to know when a storm was coming. You just started pulling everything close, bracing for what you already knew was on its way.

A THOUSAND TINY RAZOR BLADES

Nearly a year had passed since my mother's first hospitalization. I was in Mrs. Dean's fifth-grade class, and honestly, she deserved hazard pay. She stood in the front of the room, chalk in hand, trying—genuinely trying—to get through the vocabulary list without losing her mind. I sat two rows back, already grinning.

"The word 'ironic,'" she said, scanning the room. "Can someone define 'ironic'"?

My hand shot up, but I didn't wait to speak.

"It's a traffic jam when you're already late." I didn't sing it—I just said it with the exact cadence the singer, Alanis Morissette, burned into all of us with her song *Ironic*.

The class erupted in laughter; obviously, they knew the song as well. Mrs. Dean blinked, dropped the chalk into her sweater pocket, and gave me a slow nod, half acknowledgement, half prayer.

She held up a hand, her voice calm but clearly hanging by a thread. "Trey, if you use the word 'ironic' or mention anything about Alanis Morissette even one more time, I'm sending you to the office."

I nodded. Then, without missing a beat: "Well, *that's* ironic. Because if I go to the office, I'll miss class, and if I miss class, how am I supposed to pass the vocab test?"

She didn't say a word. Just pointed to the door.

I doubled over, like it was the best joke I'd ever heard. But unfortunately, it was just *one more thing* for my mom to deal with.

At home that night, I watched her cough so hard that it seemed to shake her entire body. "I'm fine," she'd say, waving off my concern, even as beads of sweat gathered around her hairline and her breath came in short, uneven bursts.

"No chills, no shaking," she'd say firmly, as if those words could convince me—or that it wasn't serious. Or that the sickness would back off if she just denied it hard enough.

My mom's doctor admitted her to the hospital again a few days later. The gown hung off her shoulders, too big, too bright against skin that had gone pale and papery. She lay there, swallowed up by the hospital bed and the room as she became the smallest thing in it.

Valentine's Day came and went without ceremony—a wilted bouquet I brought to my mom, and a tray of food cooling untouched by her bedside. She surfaced now and then, eyes half-open, her fingers brushing against mine in a slow,

searching motion. Just enough to let me know that she knew I was there. Then she'd slip back under, caught in a sleep that offered no real rest.

That time, she was in the hospital for nine days. By the fifth day, the calendar stopped mattering. At home, everything felt off. Her bedroom was untouched, too neat, too still—too paused mid-life.

I couldn't stay home overnight by myself, not yet. So if my sister, Tobilyn, couldn't make it back from college, the backup plan kicked in: my dad. He worked high up in the police department, a director who'd traded his uniform for a pressed suit.

Our family dinner usually meant him sitting across from me at the kitchen table, fork in hand, talking through a story I wasn't a part of—something about work, or discipline, or any other topic he was interested in.

I sat still, chewing like a hostage in a lunch meat commercial, waiting for him to glance up and ask something—anything—directed at me. A question about my day. A joke. A throwaway comment that indicated he noticed I was there. But I was a seat-filler in a conversation meant for someone else.

I hated how small it made me feel. How unimportant.

The pan hissed under my spatula, each pop of grease splattering like punctuation in the otherwise quiet kitchen. A trace of cumin drifted up; tacos had always been one of our things. Mom's lesson replayed in muscle memory: brown the beef, drain the grease, season last. For a moment, it felt like she was right there, watching me get it right.

His footsteps reached me before I saw him—steady, controlled, and my shoulders tensed on instinct.

He walked into the kitchen, eyes landing on the pan. "That's not how you cook ground beef," he said, not to me, but through me.

No greeting. No pause. Just that.

I didn't pause. Just turned, spatula still dripping grease, and fired back, "This is how mom does it. She showed me."

The words came out hotter than I intended—louder, too.

His jaw flexed, barely, but enough. "Trey, there's more than one way to cook ground beef. I don't understand why everything is an argument with you."

I cut him off. "Like I said—this is how mom showed me." My words shot out like bullets from a gun, "I'm cooking it this way because it's the *only* way I know. You're never here. This isn't your house!"

I felt a surge of adrenaline, and I couldn't stop myself.

He needed to hear it. Someone did. While my mom was hooked up to machines, holding on by a thread, I was here— just trying to keep something—literally anything from falling apart. I wasn't trying to win an award or argument. I was just trying not to burn dinner or cry into the taco meat, at least not at the same time.

His expression changed. First, the color drained from his face, his jaw locked so tight it looked carved in stone. A beat later, the color came flooding back. His cheeks flared red, and his voice erupted, rattling the cabinets.

"WHO DO YOU THINK PAYS FOR THIS HOUSE? I DO. This is MY house, and I'm telling YOU—there is more

than one damn way to cook meat! Just because your mom does it one way doesn't mean anything. Not everything she does is perfect!"

I gripped the spatula until my knuckles were white. I kept my eyes on the pan. I wanted to ask how much Wild Turkey whiskey he'd already polished off that day—or if he was just cranky because his flask ran dry and he needed a refill. Instead, I swallowed a thousand tiny razor blades because I couldn't say what I wanted back at him. So, nothing came out.

I turned back to the stove, pretending the sizzle of the meat was the only thing in the room. If I stayed focused on the pan, on the sound, on anything but him—maybe I could erase him.

He folded his arms, leaning back like I was a perp sitting across from him in some dingy detective's office. The overhead kitchen light cast a harsh glare, washing everything in a cold, unnatural hue that only added to the interrogation vibe:

"You know..." he said, "I lived in this house before you were even born," his voice was stiff, calculated—less a statement, more like he was laying out a case against me. Patiently waiting for me to trip up under the pressure.

Then he shrugged and said, "Oh well, Mom's not here." The words dripped with a nonchalance that made my skin crawl. It wasn't just what he said; it was the way he said it, as if none of this mattered, like she didn't matter. Like I didn't.

Our relationship felt transactional, like he was doing me a solid by simply existing in the same space, allowing me to breathe his air. There was an unspoken fine print: *I'm here because I have to be, not because I want to be.*

Anytime I pushed back, he'd twist it fast and smug—like he'd been salivating for the opening. It was his cue to climb up on his soapbox. "Well, I'm not a deadbeat dad. Lots of kids have nothing! No Christmas. No birthday presents—no child support. No house. Nothing. You're so ungrateful."

I couldn't argue with that.

He showed up on Christmas. On my birthday. And always paid child support.

But what about how I felt when I saw my mom wired to machines that helped her breathe? How about all the days that aren't special occasions?

He never asked how that felt. He didn't put his arm around me—his own son—and express any empathy in my situation.

He wasn't compassionate. It felt like he never tried.

The most he ever said was, "Well, if she'd stop smoking, she wouldn't be in the hospital."

That was his version of comfort, and I was supposed to be grateful for it.

THE DISTANCE BETWEEN THE WANT AND THE WORD

The summer before sixth grade, Atlanta caught full-blown Olympic fever. The city morphed into a chaotic obstacle course of road closures and gridlock. During the games, Mom's office worked flex hours; she had to leave the house at 4 a.m., slipping out quietly before the sun even stretched, just to get to work on time.

With no one to watch me, my mom signed the forms and packed my trunk for a Christian YMCA camp outside of Athens, Georgia. Two full weeks. To her, it looked perfect: safe, supervised, wholesome.

To me, it felt like exile.

The place looked like someone designed it after seeing

summer camps only in Hallmark movies: rolling hills, a suspiciously shiny lake, enough pine trees to launch a lumber brand. The air smelled of equal parts cut grass, expired sunscreen, and bug spray that could stun a horse. Somewhere in the distance, boys were yelling with the kind of unearned confidence only middle school athletes possess.

By day, it was chaos in cargo shorts. We tore through the woods in packs, half-warrior, half-lost-boy, chasing each other until the light gave out. The fastest way back was straight across the lake, so we piled into the rowboats and paddled like castaways in a bad adventure movie.

At night, we paused long enough for the evening service, where sweat-drenched boys tried to look pious while sneak-wiping sweat on their pew neighbors.

The youth pastor stood onstage, framed by string lights, ferns, and a dramatic row of tiki torches that gave the whole thing the vibe of a *Survivor* tribal council. He had a Bible in one hand and a microphone in the other, speaking to a crowd of about 150 of us—boys ranging from ages eight to seventeen.

"Yesterday we talked about the rapture," he began, pacing the stage. "You have to be ready. No heads up. No warning. Your parents won't whisper it before bed, your teacher won't send a note home. One second you're brushing your teeth, the next—trumpets blaring, and everyone left behind will know exactly what they missed."

Whenever the end of the world came up, a wave of heat moved through me. I was terrified of the idea of death, the finality of something gone for good. The thought that no matter what you did, it all just stopped. That everything

could simply end—was too big for my mind to hold, but I tried anyway.

"Tonight," he said, his voice lowering, "we're going to talk about the ways the devil finds his way into your heart."

From the back row, a kid yelled, "From smoking!" and the group broke in laughter, ripped through the crowd, even the youth minister cracking up before pulling himself back to his serious persona.

The youth pastor grinned like he was about to tell a joke, and obviously, he already knew the punchline. "It's pretty awesome, right?" he said. "That God created Adam and Eve in His image—and through them, created us."

The younger kids in the front row nodded, still hung up on the talking snake part. The rest of us sat waiting for the story to take a turn.

He shifted tone again, more serious now. "But Adam and Eve isn't just about where we came from. It's about temptation. Eve had the serpent. Maybe yours is sneaking candy before dinner, or cheating on a test, or lying."

A ripple of movement passed through the rows.

Kids elbowed each other, grinning, some whispering admissions that barely made it past their lips. A few nodded toward the floor, guilty smiles tugging at their faces. Every "temptation" he listed was a hit—candy, cheating, lying—we all had experienced a kind of nervous relief from realizing we were all guilty of the same things.

"Now, you know God told us to create," he said, pausing just long enough for us to inhale the silence. "Be fruitful. Multiply."

He glanced across the rows, "Two men can't do that. Neither can two women."

Then, with a smile meant to be compassionate, "God loves everyone," he began, letting the words stretch, soft and syrupy. "But He doesn't love the sin."

"See, temptation isn't who you are—it's something you fight. We all have our struggles. Some lie. Some cheat. Some... choose a different kind of sin." He continued, *"But if they let Jesus in—if they turn away from that life—He can still save them from eternal damnation."*

He didn't need to say the word. Everyone knew which "different kind" of sin he meant. The way he spoke, it sounded like God had whispered the sermon to him personally over breakfast. That alone was terrifying.

Then, I hear trumpets start before I can even register what is happening.

The first note slices through the air, enough to make a few kids flinch. My stomach drops. The swell of the trumpets builds, and for a second, everything inside me freezes. This is it—the end. Every sermon, it's all true... and I'm not ready.

A thought flashes: *I thought I had more time.*

My pulse hammers, the sound tunnels through me, ringing in my ears until it feels like it's coming from inside my own body. I looked around, hoping someone else—anyone— looked even a little disturbed. Or if anyone could tell. If they were looking in my direction, half-expecting someone to point at me and yell, "It's him!"

But no. Just me and my little gay secret, trapped in khaki

cargo shorts. I was convinced there was a flashing neon sign over my head—*Sinner, Party of One* in pretty cursive.

The trumpets cut off mid-blast.

For a beat, our little amphitheater was suspended in silence. You could hear breathing and the sound of people trying not to move.

The youth pastor climbed back onto the stage. He smiled, slow and intentional, scanning the rows of boys.

"Some of you look a little shaken," he said, voice smooth again, almost kind. "Maybe tonight's a good time to ask yourself something..." He let the pause linger, "If those trumpets had been real...and not just a recording, where would you be right now?"

I sat frozen, breath jammed somewhere between panic and puberty, knees locked to my chest like I was trying to hatch myself out of the situation. Around me, the other boys barely moved. One picked at his shoelace, another leaned back and stretched, yawning through the warning of eternal fire— no big deal.

I wanted to shake them. *Didn't they hear what he just said?*

Because I did. Every word. Each one aimed right at the part of me I'd never say out loud. I was terrified of being seen by people. Private moments. Desires I'd worked so hard to forget...

Late at night, when everything slowed down, it always found me. That pull I didn't have words for yet. It started as a spark—curiosity maybe, then something heavier—heat, heartbeat, then overwhelming guilt.

I'd try to stop it, bargain with myself, but it always won.

Always. And when it was over, I'd lie there staring at my hands as if they belonged to someone else.

That's usually when it hits, the shame. Not just for what I did, but for what it meant—for whom it said I was. I'd yank the blanket over my head, hoping God couldn't see through cotton. Which, in case you're wondering, is not the type of spiritual awakening they promise in youth group camp.

I TOLD YOU NOT TO BRING THAT DEVIL INTO MY HOUSE

Middle school summers dragged—long, hot, and quiet. Other kids had pools and cul-de-sacs. I had a busted bike, no ride, and a house marooned on a five-lane road.

Honestly, until I could drive, the highlight of my summers came after dark, I'd flick on the TV. The soft glow lit up my bedroom as the opening chords of MTV's *120 Minutes* rolled in—like a secret track just for me.

For anyone too young to remember, *120 Minutes* was this late-night music video show that played all of the weird, moody stuff you'd rarely see during the day. Think of it as the emo Internet before the Internet we know. And yes, I'm fully dating myself for saying that.

By the mid-90s, music hit me like a live wire. I found my

way into rock through The Cranberries, Oasis, No Doubt, and obviously, Alanis.

Her voice got me. One minute soft enough to sound like a confession, the next, shredding the air like she was exorcising something. It felt raw and alive and nothing like the buttoned-up world I live in. I'd sit cross-legged on the floor, eyes glued to the TV, watching her stalk the stage—hair flying, head banging, daring the mic to keep up.

My admiration for her wasn't exactly subtle. Anyone surprised I was into guys clearly hadn't been paying attention.

I fell in love with Deftones around the same time. Their sound cut through everything else—raw, hypnotic, loud. Chino Moreno's voice was a velvet-covered dagger: slipping in soft and low, then slicing clean against Stephen Carpenter's riffs. The music crawled into places I couldn't acknowledge, echoing the chaos I kept tucked away. Deftones *sounded* like all of it.

I'd lose myself in my Discman—headphones on, press play, and the first guitar riff would hit, and just take over. Music became one of the only places that felt right.

My mom never blinked at the screaming vocals or bass that rattled the walls, no matter how loud or late it got. But Marilyn Manson? Hard no.

The summer before seventh grade, a Saturday afternoon, my mom dropped us off at the mall—AC blasting in the car, but losing the war against the Georgia heat. My friend and I spilled out of the car, already scheming how we were going to spend the twenty-dollar bills burning holes in our pockets.

"Have fun," Mom called after me. "But don't come home with a Marilyn Manson CD."

The second we hit the food court, I veered straight to the music store. There it was, *Smells Like Children,* Marilyn Manson's sophomore release, basically begging me to pick it up. My hands shook like I was stealing it, but the cashier didn't care about my age. Into the bag it went—my prize.

All I remember is the sound of *Sweet Dreams* beating through my room as she appeared in the doorway.

"Hand it over," she said.

No yelling. Just a calm, cold command. I handed it over. She walked off. I ran after her.

In the kitchen, she opened a drawer. Not to hide the CD. To grab a hammer.

"Mom!"

Too late. She dropped it on the counter, lined it up like a nail, and brought the hammer down hard.

CRACK.

Plastic split, fragments flying across the counter like shrapnel. She didn't flinch. Didn't raise her voice. She kept hammering, methodically, as if she were smashing something contagious.

When the CD was nothing but shards, she wiped her hands on a dish towel, set the hammer down, and turned to me.

"I told you not to bring that devil into my house."

Then she walked away. That was the end of Marilyn Manson. And my CD.

School started in August. By the time October rolled around, I'd already received a silent lunch for talking too much during Mr. Lewis's math class. And on October 28, 1997, the hospital retook her.

This devil's name was: *persistent left lower lobe pneumonia.*

Tests started right away. Names I'd never heard before spilled out like a list of possible threats—a bronchoscopy, some kind of biopsy, something called cytology. Each one sounded worse than the last.

On October 30, Dr. Harris went in with a scope—thin tools sent down into her lungs, searching for answers in pieces of tissue pulled from deep inside her. I couldn't stop picturing it. Metal threading through her body, scraping away parts of her to be studied under glass.

When the results came back, the words were clean and clinical: no cancer, benign tissue, swelling, inflammation. But something still showed up on the scans, something in her lungs that didn't belong there.

When mom was well enough, she tried to walk the hospital hallways. But I saw it—how her steps wobbled, how fast she was breathing, like she couldn't quite catch the air she needed. As her oxygen levels dropped below 88%, the monitor let out a sharp beep. Nurses moved fast, fitting a mask over her face and rolling her in the tank.

She came home on Halloween with an oxygen machine set up at our house. Thin tubing wrapped around her cheeks, following her from room to room, and pooling at her feet.

A FENCE SOMEWHERE

I kept swinging at shadows, hoping something else would break before I did. Eighth grade marked when things began to come undone.

I had too much swirling in my head—too many feelings, too many questions, too many ways I didn't fit. It was the kind of disorientation you get when a wave hits harder than expected. One minute, you're laughing in the surf, the next you're tumbling—limbs flailing, lungs burning—straining to figure out which way is up. Every direction felt wrong. Every attempt to steady myself left me more off-balance than before.

Thirteen is its own circle of hell. No one reflects on middle school and says, "Wow, what a golden era. What a shame it's over."

No, middle school is where optimism goes to die—between awkward growth spurts (or lack thereof), cafeteria

politics, and the first time someone tells you your voice sounds weird. You feel criticized just for existing.

On top of all of that, my mom was sick. And I thought I was too—just in a different way. I believed the "thing" inside me would send me to hell. That one day, my mom would find out, and it would break her. If her body didn't give out first, the truth would.

That fear made me feel like a foreigner in my own life. I had plenty of friends, but I couldn't reach the ease with which they moved through so effortlessly. While I could study them or mimic "normal" attraction—joy, comfort, a sense of belonging—it never connected with me. It didn't click in the same way as my attraction to guys.

It was the first time I understood there was a gap between how I presented myself and what I lived. The light I gave off wasn't fake, but it wasn't the whole picture either. Not by miles.

At school, I basically had season tickets to the administrator's office. I did a lot of dumb things.

Take science class. We were learning about the mitochondria, but my attention was elsewhere. A girl in the class casually explained what a maxi pad was before the lesson started, and the only part that stuck with me was, "It works like a sticker." That was all I needed. My brain lit up like a slot machine.

I slipped her a note: *Can I have two?* She didn't ask why. She didn't even write back. She just handed them over under the desk. And while the rest of the class reviewed cell structures, I decided mitochondria could wait. I had a mission.

Hall pass in hand, I shoved the pads deep into my jean

pockets and made a beeline for the boys' bathroom. Once inside, I locked the stall and prepared for phase two:

I ripped open the packages with the urgency of someone defusing a bomb, peeled off the adhesive strips, and tossed the wrappers in the toilet—where they floated like tiny, guilty rafts.

I carried the pads back in my palms, sticky side up; every step down the hall was a prayer for no one to turn the corner. As I walked back to my class, I leapt up and slapped the pads dead-center on the hallway clocks—one on each side. Perfect placement. An absolute masterpiece.

I walked back into class with absolutely no chill. I was vibrating. It felt like Christmas Eve, but with a dash of petty vandalism. I couldn't even glance at my pad dealer. One look at her, and I'd lose it completely.

Ten minutes later, the bell rang. Doors burst open, and the hallway filled with over a hundred eighth graders. It didn't take long for someone to notice my art installation.

"Yo—why are there pads on the clock?"

Fingers pointed upward at the oversized pads, stuck like defiant little mitochondria of chaos, fueling the energy of the entire hallway.

My impromptu "art installation" didn't exactly scream maturity, but it was still glorious.

Unfortunately, school was the only outlet for all that restless energy, which meant my teachers got front-row seats to the show. The office staff knew me better than my classmates—half the time, I felt like I should've had my own desk outside the principal's door.

Detentions and in-school suspensions were annoying,

but the real trouble was the migraines. They've been around as long as I can remember. The first one hit when I was five. When the pain would start, I'd imagine a construction crew inside of my head—hard hats, steel boots, jackhammers pounding behind my eyes. It was loud, violent, and somehow worse because it was invisible to everyone else but me.

By eighth grade, the migraines came like clockwork, at least one a week. The warning sign was always the same: black auras sliding across my vision, their arrival ended my day. Around then, couples had started to form—fingers brushing together in the hallways, hushed phone calls stretching late into the night, plans for movies and football games scribbled on loose-leaf paper. At lunch, my friends dissected these secretive connections with the intensity of sports commentators—who was seen holding hands, who might kiss after Friday's game, who would likely break up before the next dance.

I didn't fully understand why, but I knew those moments weren't meant for me. Not the way they were for them. There was no roadmap for what I was feeling—only the awareness that I was already off-course.

They were falling in love. I was learning to act.

My acting out, disorientation, and pain were all connected. Different symptoms of the same thing. Anger, mostly. But underneath that, if I'm being honest, sadness.

Anger felt easier to carry. More acceptable. It made me feel powerful, even if it was a lie. Sadness required something I didn't have yet: permission. Vulnerability. I understood that, even then. It didn't fix anything. It just played out the questions I'd never have answers to.

What's wrong with me?

Why can't I stop?

Why doesn't anyone notice how much it hurts?

Teachers started speaking to me like a problem they'd already tried to solve.

At home, my mom's eyes tracked me with that tight, tired mix of worry and frustration.

And me? I was just trying not to fall apart during the first period. Or do something so dumb it would earn me another trip to the principal's office.

The part of my life I wanted to ignore somehow became national news and ended up everywhere. Suddenly, everyone had an opinion about homosexuality. Everyone had an opinion about a young man in Wyoming.

The first time I heard his name, I was in the living room with my mom. The TV washed the carpet in cold blue light. Everything else was still:

"Gay man. Tied to a fence. Beaten."

His name was Matthew Shepard.

I stole a glance at my mom—watching for her reaction.

Did she hear it the way I did?

How did she react to that word...*gay?*

Could she see it on me?

The TV suddenly broadcast the truth I'd worked so hard to bury across our living room, and it felt like a rainbow lit across my forehead.

Neither of us said a word. But I swear, even the furniture was avoiding eye contact.

None of it mattered. My mind had slipped—past the

couch, past the walls—out there, in the middle of that desolate Wyoming field, where Matthew Shepard had been tied to a fence and left for dead.

His murder didn't feel like some distant tragedy happening to someone else. It wasn't just his name or his story; it was the possibility of my own.

It was me.

And it hadn't come out of nowhere. The same threat that found Matthew on that quiet stretch of road—that hatred—lived everywhere. It moved through locker rooms, classrooms, and church pews. The same hate that had tied him to that fence and left him there.

It didn't hide. It didn't have to.

So I took the hint and reorganized a little further back into the closet.

By December, my parents—two people who could barely agree on what day it was—somehow landed on the same conclusion: I needed help. My behavior was "out of control."

Fine. Therapy wasn't new. I'd already done the circuit—plush office chairs, pretty bubbling aquariums meant to coax you into spilling your guts, the soft gurgle of the pump filtering the water in the same way I always did with doctors. With all their questions:

"How did it make you feel that your dad left?"

"That your mom was sick?"

"That you are wasting all of your potential?"

All very thoughtful—if you were aiming a mile wide and an inch deep.

And then there was Ridgeview Institute. The name landed like an anvil in a cartoon. All that was missing was the whistle on the way down. I'd overheard it before, in hushed conversations meant to stay out of my earshot. I knew it wasn't like any of the places I'd been before—diffusers pumping out lavender oil and walls plastered with laminated quotes about blooming when you are planted.

Ridgeview carried a different energy. A psychiatric facility. A place for people who'd run out of other options.

"Your dad's meeting us there," my mom said finally, with the cadence of something practiced, because she wanted to get through it fast.

The fact that they were both involved in this told me everything I needed to know.

My mom's hands locked around the steering wheel, her knuckles drained of their color against the leather. I kept firing off questions, and local 99X played some angsty alt-rock track, but even the guitars felt quieter than usual.

The car turned into Ridgeview's driveway—too smooth, too clean, and working too hard to convince you it was a good idea. The trees lined the curve looked like props, set design for a place pretending to be inviting.

My dad's car was already there, parked off to the side. I stared at the windshield, half-expecting to see him inside, tapping his fingers on the steering wheel, already halfway to frustration. For a second, I wondered if he and my mom had actually talked—really talked—on anything beyond logistics? Was I there because I reminded them of the guy on the news?

Mom eased into a space and turned off the engine. "Let's go." Her voice steady but soft.

I stepped out of the car, the cool December air barreling towards my skin as I glanced toward the entrance. The building seemed bigger now, closer, its clean lines and muted colors no longer inviting but indifferent.

My dad nodded when we reached him, but didn't say anything, and neither did she. Whatever uneasy alliance they'd struck to get me here didn't extend to small talk.

The psychiatrist greeted us with professional warmth, polished by years of training and repetition. His handshake was genuine enough to seem sincere without inviting connection. Behind him, a wall of bookshelves held thick, serious volumes, their spines aligned with unsettling precision. The lighting worked hard to soften the space, but it couldn't quite smooth

over the authority decorated into the room. His desk made sure of that—dark, glossy, and probably with its own PhD.

The session started like all the others. The psychiatrist ran through the usual checklist—school, friends, my hyperactive behavior, calmly adjusting his glasses as he scribbled notes and deciphering some secret message I had no idea I was sending.

The psychiatrist then nodded along while my parents filled in the blanks I would have preferred to leave blank.

"Problems with authority," "obsessive compulsive patterns," "impulse control"—these clinical terms tossed about. They talked about me like I was just some abstract documentary they'd just watched.

I sat there thinking, *Wow, fascinating stuff—someone should really check in on that kid.*

And then it happened.

No lean-in whisper or furrowed brow.

Just calm, clinical delivery: "I think it's in Trey's best interest, " the doctor stated, speaking so casually you'd think he was about to recommend a change in shampoo, "to admit him here for inpatient treatment."

For a second, I genuinely looked around the room to see who else he might be talking about.

"Wait. What?"

The words flew out, my voice cracking like I'd started puberty all over again. I sat up straight, fully alert now.

"You mean...now? Like, right now?"

The psychiatrist nodded, "I believe it's necessary."

Cool. Great, I thought. Just how perfect. Surprise

institutionalization was at the top of my Christmas list this year.

Necessary? Inpatient therapy? Now? The words didn't make sense, didn't belong in the same conversation I'd been having five minutes ago. I'd just lost a game I didn't know I was even playing.

"But Christmas is two weeks away!" I stammered. My voice jumped an octave without asking permission. "You just—I mean, I can't—I sat there, blinking at the doctor, waiting for someone, anyone to say this was all a big misunderstanding.

Even worse—my parents didn't just come up with this. It wasn't some "maybe we should" idea tossed into the room. The plan was set. A done deal. They'd driven me here knowing I wouldn't be going home.

I looked at the door, wondered how fast I'd have to be to make it out. But my body didn't get the memo. It turns out, "fight or flight" also includes "completely freeze." I was not the one deciding. They checked me in like luggage. And everyone seemed weirdly okay with that.

The main entrance to the inpatient building we went to next tried really hard to make us feel safe. It led to an aggressively neutral room. Accented pastel walls. Plants. Cheerful throw pillows. Furniture arranged like a Pottery Barn catalog with abandonment issues. It was giving "hope," but in a way that felt mass-produced—like someone tried to decorate their way out of institutional trauma.

Sunlight poured through oversized windows, casting golden patches across the overly polished floor. The ceilings stretched high—cathedral-esque, hoping their grandeur

might distract us from the fact that no one here was actually free to leave.

But I knew better. It was too perfect. It felt like every corner had been cleaned by someone trying to erase a crime scene. I wanted to believe the illusion. I really did.

WHO I WAS BROKE MORE RULES THAN WHAT THEY DID

By the time they showed me to my sleeping quarters, the anger had calcified. The room was expansive and clinical—rows of identical cots spaced just far enough apart to feel intentional, but not enough to offer privacy.

Everything buzzed: the lights, the tensions, the part of me that still couldn't believe I was here. The security camera in the corner had grown numb from watching this on repeat. I gave it a nod—the camera, and I were both trapped in the same terrible sitcom.

My assigned cot was near the middle—just as impersonal as the rest. It was thin enough to qualify as a suggestion rather than support. Someone tucked the corners of the blanket with such sterile precision that the gesture felt pointless.

I sat down. Slowly. The cot let out a dramatic squeak, as if it were judging me for being there. I took it personally, then pretended that I didn't, as I traced the soulless grid of the room looking for signs of life.

Sleep felt fictional. Something that happened for other people, not under clinical lighting and monitored like they're in the NICU.

Then came the nurse.

She moved through the room—with the practiced hush of someone accustomed to being ignored and obeyed. Her footsteps were soft, choreographed, and almost bored.

She paused at each cot, taking pulses and logging vitals like we were inventory items. When she reached mine, I tensed.

Her hand pressed against my wrist—procedural, cold, all function. I could have been a chair for all she noticed. She read off my vitals in a tone usually reserved for printer settings—impersonal, efficient, and halfway done with me.

The days ran on rails—every hour pre-assigned, every movement accounted for. No detours. No shortcuts. Staff offered rewards like bait: behave, comply, earn five extra minutes of fake freedom. Trust didn't give trust; it felt rationed, and only if you played the part.

Even showering came with a set of rules—and just enough humiliation to remind you who was in charge. The first time I stepped into the bathroom, I froze. The nurse—a man in his late thirties with an expression that suggested he had seen it all—stood just outside the open door. The shower curtain, thin and translucent, was my only defense. My skin crawled as I turned the faucet, the lukewarm water hitting my back and doing nothing to wash away the feeling of eyes just beyond the veil.

I wasn't a person anymore. I was a patient.

The realization hit me every time I moved, every time I opened my mouth to speak, and saw someone jot something down in a notebook. My thoughts weren't mine; they were dissected in real time, translated into observations and outcomes. My existence had become a chart, a series of metrics to be monitored and managed. In this place, I wasn't allowed to be anything more than what they decided I was.

Group therapy was a parade of wounds—some fresh, some worn-in. The circle was always a strange mix, filled with kids who ranged from eleven to sixteen, though age didn't seem to matter here. At thirteen, I floated between roles—sometimes the youngest and other times the oldest.

The stories didn't start with words. They lived in their folded arms—pulled across their chests, tight like armor. In how their eyes stayed low, as if making eye contact might break them open.

Within the first fifteen minutes of intros, I'd learned some were shuffled through the foster system, passed around like worn-out hand-me-downs—each transfer eroding a little more of their trust. Others had been expelled from schools, their names buried in files that no one would ever open again. A fresh few were out of juvie, for violence, drugs, or both.

Across from me sat a boy, maybe two years older— though he looked like life had aged him ahead of schedule. He slumped low and folded awkwardly into the chair. Angry

clusters of acne inflamed his skin, hair stringy and slick with grease. He didn't twitch in his seat or fidget like some of the other kids did when the silence stretched too long. He simply sat there: a shadow occupying space without fully being in it.

He'd been caught with a knife at school, again. The year before, he'd pulled one on another kid. When the school found the knife, their response was automatic: straight to youth detention, then here. Ridgeview was Stop Two on a conveyor belt that didn't seem to slow down.

What stuck with me was the part he felt most angry about. It was the knife. Losing it. That was the part he couldn't hide. I watched him from the other side of the circle, trying to understand how someone could hold so much emptiness and still take up space.

One of the girls traced the scar along her forearm as she spoke of her father—more storm than man. Always breaking things. By eleven, she was drinking to keep the noise out. Pills followed. Next to her, a boy recounted a fight with another kid—said it seemed like a good idea at the time. He never liked the way that kid looked at him anyway.

For once in my life, I was the quiet one—amongst a group of kids whose pain wore too many faces to track. I hadn't thrown punches or put anyone in a coma. My damage wasn't the type you could point toward—I didn't have the courtesy of visible wounds.

Aside from a few outliers, their stories—the fights, the drugs, the stealing—sounded curable. Fixable. If I'd robbed a gas station or set something on fire, at least there would've been a court date, maybe even a redemption arc.

How do you fix something you can't say out loud?

There was no manual, no hotline, no "coming out of existential dread" checklist. Just me, stuck in the punchline of a joke no one else knew I was telling.

My deepest struggle wasn't what I'd done—it was who I was, which felt a little unfair, honestly. I hadn't even done anything fun to end up in crisis. It was 1998, and the only things I knew about being gay came from slogans and scare tactics. There was the Defense of Marriage Act, which sounded like it should involve tanks, and the "Ex-Gay" movement, which promised you could pray the gay away, as if it were a bad case of malaria.

According to my world, homosexuality was sinful but fixable—kind of like a bad haircut—embarrassing, temporary, and apparently curable if you just prayed hard enough. Marriage was "One Man + One Woman," ideally photographed next to a barn in coordinating denim, while TV ads showed happy nuclear families smiling under fluttering flags.

So the truth sat just under my skin, twitching like a muscle I couldn't relax.

I couldn't tell them. I couldn't tell anyone. Not about the nights I lay flat on my back, eyes locked on the ceiling fan, ashamed of where my mind had gone. Private detours I could barely admit to myself—I couldn't tell them how dirty it made me feel.

I couldn't tell this group—not when half of them had rap sheets, and the other half looked like they were still deciding which felony to commit first. I couldn't tell them

that I prayed every night for God to take it away, only to wake up unchanged. That I'd come out of dreams stained with shame—details bonding to my thoughts long after I opened my eyes.

I definitely couldn't tell them. Not this part.

The part where the world made me feel both dangerous and invisible at once. Where every slogan screamed "family values" while quietly marking me as the thing they needed protection from.

I still said grace at dinner. I still apologized when someone else bumped into me. So maybe I was just confused. Perhaps I needed to pray harder, scrub my thoughts cleaner, walk straighter—literally.

Because whatever I was, it couldn't be the thing everyone warned me about.

I didn't feel like a threat.

I felt devout enough to beg God for mercy, terrified enough to believe I needed it, and just aware enough to know I was coming undone.

So I stayed quiet.

2904

I watched my mom fold over halfway up the driveway, one hand pressed to her hip, the other grabbing the edge of the mailbox like it might steady the world. Her breath came in staccato bursts, sharp and shallow. She stood there trying to catch it, jaw tight, skin the color of week-old linen.

She straightened up slowly when she saw me watching. Forced a smile. "It's nothing," she said, waving me off with the same practiced ease she used for telemarketers and bad news.

Her voice was raspy, a little too light, like it might give out if she leaned on it. "You don't need to worry about me."

But I did. Her body was screaming the truth her words kept trying to bury.

August 21, 1999, is welded into my memory. Not a scar. Not a highlight. Just permanent. That whole summer had been leading to one thing: Alanis Morissette's stop in Atlanta on the 5½ Weeks Tour.

My best friend and I had planned for it like it was the second coming. It was also the last Saturday before high school started. Everything in my life felt like it was about to flip into something new. I should've been electric with anticipation.

And I was—until the day buckled in a way I didn't see coming.

Mom hadn't gotten up once. For someone who usually couldn't sit still long enough to finish a cup of coffee, that said everything. Her body sank deep into the mattress as if she'd surrendered to it. When her eyes opened, they found mine. She smiled, barely. The kind adults give when they're lying to kids and hoping they'll buy it.

But I wasn't five anymore. And that look didn't feel safe. It felt wrong. Off. It scared me in a way I hadn't felt before.

I checked on her constantly. Sometimes I didn't even step all the way in—just paused in the doorway long enough to watch her chest rise and fall. Proof she was still in there.

When she needed to use the bathroom, I moved on instinct. I slid an arm under her shoulder, already bracing for the collapse. The second her feet touched the floor, her knees buckled. She gripped me like furniture—tight at first, then lighter, once she found her footing.

Her legs jerked forward, stiff and slow. Each step looked like a bad idea she was going to do anyway. Ten feet to the bathroom might as well have been ten miles.

Back in bed, she sank into the pillow as her whole body exhaled. Her lips parted—just barely. "Sweetheart...they'll be there for me. They'll take you," she whispered. She started to smile, then let it go.

I waited for her to finish, standing still, watching her fade deeper into the pillow. Just breathing looked like work.

She'd arranged for two of her coworkers to take me to the concert. "I can't argue with you, Trey," she said, her voice thin but determined. "Please. Just do as I ask. They'll pick you up at five."

I couldn't sit. I drifted from room to room with no intention, arms crossing and uncrossing, as if my body kept trying to decide how to hold itself together. My feet would stall, but my thoughts didn't—they collided, scattered, each one louder than the last, and none of them clear.

I didn't even realize I was crying until the tears hit my shirt. No sobs, no sharp inhale—just tears falling like they'd been stacking up, waiting for permission. I lowered myself onto the couch, palms pressed into my face, not to block anything out but to hold myself in.

Then I heard a dragging noise.

I turned—slowly—and saw her in the hallway.

She was bracing the wall with one shoulder, barely standing, as if gravity had made a deal with her body, it was planning to break—a dancer performing her final act. She didn't speak. She didn't need to.

The words shot out of me before I had time to soften them. "Why are you up? Why didn't you use the bell?"

Her lips were faintly blue. The skin around her eyes had a dull, bruised tint. Her fingers, pale and unsteady, were the same washed-out color as her mouth.

Mom hadn't gotten up to be strong or to prove a point. She'd gotten up because she couldn't call for me.

She'd been suffocating in that room alone while I sat on the couch sobbing into my hands, convinced I was the one breaking.

Every late-night scramble, every argument, every moment I thought I was the one holding it all together—none of it mattered. Mom hadn't needed discipline or protection. She needed air.

And I hadn't seen it.

"Mom, can you breathe?"

The question barely escaped, shredded by sobs that rattled my chest.

I pulled her onto the couch. Her lips moved, forming words that never came. She was trying to say she was fine, but her skin was turning a sickening shade of blue—deeper by the second.

It reminded me of Violet Beauregarde in *Willy Wonka*, right after she chews the forbidden gum and swells into a giant blueberry—except this wasn't a movie. Just the warmth draining from my mother's face, being replaced by that same cold blue, inching across her skin on a mission.

My fingers locked around the cordless phone. I hit 911.

"Please," I begged, breathless. "Tell them to hurry. Please—just save my mom."

I didn't know what else to say. So I kept begging.

"What's your address?"

"2904." My voice cracked. "Two-nine-zero-four." I repeated it again and again, the numbers tumbling out like a prayer, as if saying them fast enough might drag the ambulance out of the sky.

It felt like hours before they arrived.

Then—the door flew open—boots on hardwood.

An EMT dropped to his knees beside her. "How long has she been this blue?" he asked, already fitting the oxygen mask over her face. His voice was steady, clinical. No small talk. Just triage.

They worked fast—silent, well-rehearsed choreography. A stretcher appeared, and within seconds, they were rolling her through the doorway, out of our house, into flashing lights.

At the ER, a nurse clipped a pulse oximeter to her finger. The monitor blinked red: 33.

Most people hover between 95 and 100. That's normal. That's safe.

She was at 33. Not normal. Not safe.

At that point, it's not a measurement—it's a countdown.

She wasn't breathing, not really. She was gasping in stutters. She didn't look alive. She looked like something had pulled her in from far away.

The next day at the hospital, I stopped in the doorway of the ICU.

The hall stretched in both directions—too clean, too bright. Machines beeped behind closed doors. The sounds bounced off tile and metal and settled into my chest, one uneven beat after another.

Before I stepped into her room, I found the hallway sink. Turned the faucet until the knob jammed full open. Boiling water hit my hands and kept going. I let it. It gave me something definite to focus on.

Then the mask. I eased it over my face. Required for her

safety—but I needed the distance too—just a layer between me and the reality waiting inside.

I opened the door.

Suddenly, my lungs stopped cooperating.

My mom lay motionless, surrounded by wires and tubing that snaked from machines into her body. Her chest rose and fell on cue, perfectly timed with the hiss and click of the ventilator.

She was there, but only in form. Her body stayed alive because the machines said so. Everything else—the part that made her her—felt out of reach.

There wasn't time to fall apart.

Whatever I felt had to wait. My mom couldn't speak for herself, and no one else was there to step in. It was on me.

I'd been learning how to do this since I was a kid—how to ask the right questions, how to sit across from adults and sound like I belonged there. Because when it came to her, there was no room for hesitation.

I used to study my sister—how calm she stayed, how her words landed exactly where she aimed them. People listened. She never fumbled. She had the kind of presence that filled a room, and people gave her the benefit of the doubt without making her earn it.

She was everything I wasn't—older, wiser, graceful, always sure of what to say. I copied what I could—practiced her voice in my own mouth. Tried to stand the way she did, shoulders squared, answers ready.

It never quite fit. But I did my best. It was all I had.

And for that room, on that day, it had to be enough.

The visit was brief.

Her eyelids fought to lift, slow under sedation, and for a second—just one—her eyes found mine. They didn't lock on, didn't track me. But something flickered—a faint recognition, dull at the edges but still there.

Her fingers twitched beneath the blanket. Barely. The kind of movement you could miss if you weren't looking for it.

But I saw it. And I knew.

She was reaching for me the only way she could.

"I love you, Mom. I'll be back tomorrow," I said, leaning in close. The words barely made a sound next to the machine.

On my way out, a nurse waved the doctor down. He turned and caught my eye. He knew who I was.

That look—that brief pause—told me everything.

"You're her son?" he asked.

I nodded. My mouth was too dry to form words to answer.

"Yes." It barely made it out.

He didn't hesitate. Didn't ease into it.

"There's a fifty-fifty chance she won't make it out of the ICU," he said. "She's very sick."

He didn't need to say more. My brain filled in the rest on its own.

I stood there nodding, barely breathing, already bracing for what might come next.

I was only fourteen.

What kind of kid plans a funeral before he even starts high school?

THE MONSTER
HAS A NAME

Bat somehow she made it. She crawled her way out of the ICU, again—defying odds with that mix of prayer and sheer will that felt stitched into her DNA. The doctors called it recovery. I knew better. It was a miracle.

Back at home, my mom had an oxygen machine keeping her alive. I had dial-up and a chat window. Some nights, it felt like we were fighting for the same thing—to breathe. Down the hall, her machine hissed and gurgled; in the den, the modem screamed for a signal.

As a walking millennial cliché, I basically treated AOL Instant Messenger like a full-time job. Back then, AIM was our social currency: cryptic away messages, overly dramatic status updates, and screen names that aged worse than frosted tips. My generation was very much online, with zero supervision and a dial-up modem connection (rendering the home's single landline connection useless for phone conversations), which we'd fight our parents over.

One night, before the end of my freshman year, a message popped up from a screen name I didn't recognize.

The messenger told me he was about to turn sixteen. I'd just turned fifteen. He said he liked Deftones and Alanis too, which instantly felt like a secret handshake. We started swapping favorite deep cuts, B-sides, and before I knew it, we weren't talking about music anymore. For a second, it felt like we were the same person, just living in different rooms.

Something in the way he wrote—quick, funny, a little bold—made me feel seen in a way most people at school never did. Then a question with the word gay blinked onto the screen—casual in its wording and anything but small.

He asked me if we had any gay people at my school.

My fingers hovered over the keyboard, frozen. The monitor in front of me was a beige, boxy Gateway beast—deep enough to double as a built-in breakfast nook. The fourteen-inch glass screen curved slightly at the edges, casting a pale glow that made everything around it appear vaguely sick.

No ellipses. No typing bubble. Just a blinking cursor with me staring at that word, afraid that answering just might detonate it and take out the entire house.

Eventually, I started typing. Slowly. Hesitantly. Then deleting and then typing again.

When I finally hit send, my hands were sweating. I told him I didn't know anyone who was gay. That was technically true. And also not the whole truth.

He responded a few minutes later, saying he'd had "gay" thoughts but didn't know what they meant. He wasn't sure what to call those feelings—or himself.

We kept going. One cautious message at a time. Each one a little braver than the last. We traded secrets like we might at a sleepover, testing the edges of what felt safe to say.

And then I typed it.

I might be, too.

I read the sentence five times. Then I sent it.

And there it was out in the world. Or at least, blinking on the other side of a chat window—half a confession, half a question, and terrifying either way.

It was the first time I said it out loud—even if "out loud" only meant tapping keys in a dim communal room lit only by a Gateway monitor. And he didn't flinch. He stayed.

Two strangers on the opposite sides of a screen, typing out the things we were too scared to say anywhere else. For once, I didn't feel defective.

Just human.

Between classes the next day, my friend, Lola, and another friend pulled me aside in the hallway. "Were you online last night?" she asked, casually, but obviously probing— something was off.

I said yes, still not sure why they were asking.

They exchanged a glance, then Lola spoke up.

"We saw your screen name," she said.

I blinked, not sure I'd heard her right.

"It was us," she went on. "We were the ones messaging you."

The words came slowly, circling first—like mosquitoes

looking for a place to land. Then one by one, they found skin, coming for blood.

That's when the hallway tilted a little.

"Is there something you want to tell us, Trey?"

My brain stalled, trying to rearrange what they said into something that didn't mean what I knew they did. I kept my expression flat, but I could feel the heat crawl up my neck. My mouth stayed shut, my body frozen in place, but everything in me wanted out.

It was bigger than anger. It wasn't fear. It was worse—someone saw what I'd spent years trying to suppress. They took something fragile, something I hadn't even figured out how to make peace with—and turned it into entertainment. I'd let my guard down, and the audience had already been seated. Worse, they were people I knew. People I thought would protect me.

That's the moment I stopped believing my friends were safe.

They said it wasn't meant to be cruel—they just wanted me to be "real." As if baiting me into confessing the thing I was most afraid of was some kind of favor. Maybe they believed that. Perhaps that made them feel better.

Which was a prettier story than the truth. They didn't have noble intentions or some higher purpose; they were just bitchy teenage girls with a computer and no supervision at a sleepover. And since I wasn't there—because, well, I have a penis, they turned on me. Ganged up. Found a new game to play.

It turned into my own private Crucible—minus the

bonnets, plus the AIM transcript and a jury of teenage girls—full-blown Salem witch trials bullshit.

They thought I'd laugh it off or even come out.

I was fifteen. We never spoke about it again. I shoved that memory down so deep, as if it never happened.

But other shit kept on coming.

A year later, during my sophomore year of high school, my mom's doctor didn't bother with euphemisms. His notes said everything: "She is miserable."

By late October 2000, my mom couldn't walk across the room without her oxygen dipping to 86%. Even just pouring a glass of water, she'd pause to steady herself, gripping the counter for balance. She was admitted to the ICU again.

She didn't cry. Didn't yell. Just sat on the edge of the exam table, staring at the wall, as it might offer a way out. When she finally spoke, her voice fell flat from exhaustion, "I just don't want to keep going through this."

The X-rays showed what her body had been trying to tell us for years: both lungs clouded in a "ground glass appearance," with the film catching what she couldn't breathe through. For five years, the scarring kept spreading. Her lungs were deteriorating; nothing helped. We didn't even have a name for what was killing her.

That all changed in November when results from her open lung biopsy came back. The local doctors couldn't make sense of it, so they sent the slides off to Mayo Clinic in Minnesota. A piece of my mom, sealed in a container, flown somewhere colder, waiting for strangers to give a diagnosis.

After years of guessing, the Mayo Clinic gave it shape.

The monster finally got a name: *Bronchiolitis Obliterans Organizing Pneumonia*—or BOOP, for short. Leave it to a disease that tried to kill my mom to come with a name that sounded almost cute, even cartoonish—but it isn't.

It's a rare lung condition in which the smallest airways and air sacs fill with scar tissue and inflammation, blocking the free flow of oxygen. Instead of healing after an illness or irritation, the lungs keep reacting, almost like they forget to stop fighting. The "organizing" part refers to the body's failed attempt to repair itself—her lungs were trying to rebuild, but instead created more damage.

Even with a diagnosis, the cause stayed out of reach—autoimmune, maybe. Connective tissue disorder? No one could say for sure. All we knew was that it was chronic and unpredictable. Doctors explained that her immune system was already threadbare, worn down from years of fighting battles never fully won.

After that hospital stay, her doctors stopped sugarcoating things. Full-time work was out. They laid out her new limits like a prescription: four days a week, six hours a day, only after easing in—slowly. She started taking Prednisone, too, a steroid meant to jolt her failing immune system into action by reducing inflammation enough to keep her lungs functioning. But the trade-off showed up fast.

Prednisone gave her breath, but took everything else. It cranked the volume on her moods, her temperature, her body—turning her into someone the medicine could manage but she couldn't recognize.

By December, her face had rounded and swelled. I'd catch

glimpses of her in the kitchen light and have to look twice, searching for the version I knew by heart.

She couldn't sit still. One minute she was refolding clean laundry, the next she was at the sink, scrubbing it with a kind of panic behind her eyes—as if she stopped, something worse might catch her. Her fingers twitched, hands shaky. She'd snap at a squeaky cabinet door or an uneven towel edge like they'd called her a bad mother.

My mom didn't curse—at least not casually. If a four-letter word slipped out, it was because she'd dropped something on her foot or scorched her hand pulling a pan from the oven. It was reserved for pain, not regular conversation. Her go-to was a drawn-out "shhhttt"—no "i," just enough sound to release whatever she was holding in.

I still remember the first time I heard her say "fuck." It stopped time. That word coming out of her mouth felt wrong, not in a moral sense, but like watching a dog meow. It didn't fit. It wasn't her.

When her short-term disability benefits ran out, the paychecks shrank—but support didn't. Her colleagues stepped in without announcement, passing around a form, signing their names, donating their unused vacation hours to cover the gap. They gave up their own time off so she wouldn't lose her whole paycheck.

She'd return to full-time hours within less than a year.

The hospital took her back not long after.

Red strobes bounced off the house across the street, each flash throwing our front yard into a war zone of darkness and light.

She couldn't catch her breath.

By then, I should've been used to it—the paramedics flooding in, the emotional rollercoaster, and the questions they asked. The third time doesn't make it easier; it just strips away the surprise. They loaded my mom into the ambulance, doors closing with a finality I'd stopped reacting to.

In the waiting room, the chair felt colder than it should've...like it was tired of me showing up.

The doctors spoke quietly. Very high chance of a "pulmonary embolism," one of them said. He said it with a certainty that made me hate him on sight. A clot in her lungs. An ambush we didn't see coming.

Emergency Room doctors ordered a pulmonary arteriogram—a scan to trace the blood's path and see where it stopped. Dye was injected into her bloodstream so they could watch how it moved through her lungs, like tracing traffic patterns in a city.

The results came back—no embolism. For a second, relief hit, brief and blinding, before it disappeared just as fast. Her oxygen levels wouldn't hold. The BOOP had done its work; her lungs were only half-participating, expecting the rest of her body to handle what they couldn't.

They decided to intubate. The ventilator would breathe for her, forcing air in when her body refused to. Without the machine forcing air in, her blood oxygen would dip to dangerous levels, and they were concerned about organ failure.

She was fifty-one, but some days her body acted twice that. Getting out of bed required a plan. Standing too quickly left her winded, her hand gripping the bed rail until the

room settled. After nearly three weeks in the hospital, her pulmonologist, Dr. Bruce, stopped offering choices. Retire now, she said, or risk not seeing me graduate high school. Another BOOP flare could finish what the last one started.

For my mom, stepping away wasn't just about losing a paycheck; it was losing ground she'd spent years clawing her way across.

She'd built a career from nothing. Brick by brick. From nights counting change for toilet paper to becoming a Division Director in less than a decade. It was her proof. Her way of saying that divorce, illness, and single motherhood hadn't written her story for her.

And now, she had to hand it all back.

What she'd earned in her retirement pension wasn't much—hardly enough to keep a sixteen-year-old afloat. Georgia state employees didn't exactly retire into luxury, especially not at fifty-one.

But my mom wasn't built for surrender. She hired an attorney, pored over every clause and footnote until she found a way through. There was a clause that let her buy back the years she'd stepped away to raise my sister and me.

So she did.

The cover letter tucked inside my mom's Disability Retirement Application, filed in December 2001, felt like a eulogy.

Her account specialist wrote it, someone who'd shared hallways and coffee breaks with my mom for over a decade. In two short paragraphs, she captured something I couldn't articulate at the age of sixteen.

Establishing the tone with just four words, it began with "On a personal note…I worked with Ms. Toler for 10 years at the Employee Retirement System. During that time, she received several promotions, going from the initial position of temporary general secretary to finally reaching a level of Division Director."

I had to read the last line twice.

Division Director.

I knew where she had come from and what she had pushed through. I'd watch her rebuild from rubble more than once. But seeing it spelled out—what she accomplished, not as my mother, but as a professional—was incredible.

"This indicates a high level of ability, skill, and dependability," the letter continued—and then the part that cracked me open:

"Never, in all the time we worked together until the onset of her illness, did she shirk any task or duty. Even after becoming chronically ill, she continued to make every effort to continue working until it became painfully apparent to all that she just could not continue as before."

That final sentence didn't need dressing up. It was clear, final, and full of grace.

I pictured my mom at her desk, typing through deadlines while her body was at war. The oxygen tank she wheeled beside her in those final months, trying to make it look like just another piece of office equipment.

She never asked for special treatment or accommodations—not even when she could barely breathe.

She didn't complain.

She just kept showing up—oxygen tank, chronic fatigue, and all.

She made it impossible to ignore her strength.

My mother was an absolute badass.

TWO CRISIS CENTERS, ONE BODY

As adults, we get good at storage. We take the things that scare us, shame us, or still sting and tuck them away—sealed tight in mental boxes labeled *deal with later*.

And trust me, mine's packed to capacity. There's a box marked *Middle School Haircut Choices*—locked tight because no one needs to relive my grocery-store box bleach era. Somewhere nearby, there's a shoebox called *Why Did I Say That Out Loud?* That one gets new inventory daily.

But kids don't have that luxury. They feel everything in real time—grief, guilt, hope, stacked on top of each other with no room to breathe. There's no filing cabinet for sorting, no sense that any of it will pass. When something hurts, it feels permanent. When something breaks, it feels final.

I wasn't inherently negative. I wanted to believe things would work out—most days, I did. But normal never stayed long. My mom would recover, we'd catch our breath, and for a while it almost felt steady again. Then something else would crash through, resetting everything.

Hope became a reflex, but so did bracing for impact.

My adolescent years felt like someone tossed me the responsibilities of a forty-year-old and said, "Good luck, champ." While my friends stressed over algebra tests, I was counting the pills in my mom's weekly organizer, checking and rechecking the doses, a test I couldn't afford to fail.

Caregiving rewired me. I learned to speak the language of adults long before I ever felt like one—tracking oxygen levels, memorizing prescriptions, translating doctor-speak into something my mom could process when she was heavily medicated. I could sound steady when she needed calm, older when the room demanded authority.

It came with a price. I kept slipping between worlds that didn't make sense together. One minute, I was managing medication lists, the next slouching at a desk at school. Somewhere between cafeteria gossip and ventilator updates, I was also a kid praying no one figured out I was gay. Then I'd flip through my Bible and wonder how something that gave me peace could also make me feel condemned in my own skin.

So I spent half my time trying to pray the gay away and the other half pretending I didn't know what that meant. Layered on top of caregiving and the closet, my parents gifted me an array of other adult issues stacked on my back like a Jenga tower ready to tip. Things I had no business carrying as a child.

There were a lot of hats for one head, and none of them fit right.

We didn't have the instant access kids do now. No TikTok therapists breaking down trauma in sixty seconds. Back then, if you were lost, you stayed that way. There wasn't a feed full of people confessing the same secrets you were scared to say out loud.

I didn't know how to handle any of it. I just knew I had to.

Now, I'm at the age where people start using phrases like "sandwich generation." Caught between managing aging parents and holding up whoever's leaning on you next. Everyone's trading advice about burnout, estate planning, and emotional boundaries—it feels like a group project we all forgot was due.

At least as adults, we've built up a callus or two. We've learned the road zigzags. You expect detours, the phone calls that start with "You should sit down." You know which specialists to call, how to decode insurance claims, how to nod through meetings, answer emails, and pretend you're not standing in the middle of your own slow-motion emergency.

Imagine being twelve. Or fifteen—with no manual, no backup plan, just a kid troubleshooting adult problems with the confidence of someone who'd only ever fixed a paper jam.

And who was ever going to understand any of that? I'd sit across from friends, nodding at their stories about weekend plans, sports, or crushes, and the words I carried stayed sealed behind my teeth. Even if I tried, what could I say that would make sense to them? They weren't supposed to know how it felt. Their biggest emergencies were bad report cards and

missed curfews. Mine came with paramedics and possibly eternal damnation.

One afternoon, I came home from school, backpack still hanging off one shoulder, and found Mom at the kitchen table. She sat quietly, a small pile of medical supplies in front of her, the wrappers unopened in her trembling hands.

Without a word, I went to the sink. I washed my hands the way I'd watched the nurses do and dried them on the dish towel. When I sat down beside her, she handed me the tape.

"Go slow," she whispered.

I peeled it back inch by inch. She flinched. I muttered an apology. She gave me the same answer she always did—"It's okay"—even when it wasn't.

The incision cut across her side, pink and stubborn, still learning how to close. I followed the steps the nurse had shown me—clean, dry, replace. Fresh gauze, steady hands. The smell of antiseptic mixed with detergent from her shirt. When I pressed the tape down, it stuck to my fingers before it held to her skin.

I was still wearing my backpack when I finished, she said, "Thank you, Trey—I don't know what I'd do without you."

She meant it, and she was right. There was literally no one else to do it *but* me.

I tossed the wrappers into the trash, rewashed my hands, and let the water run longer than I needed to. My backpack finally dropped on the ground somewhere by the table. Somewhere else, my friends were sprawled on couches, running laps at practice, shouting over video games, or laughing about nothing. My afternoons didn't sound like theirs.

I was running two crisis centers out of the same body.

It felt like being your own parent, nurse, and PR rep—all before I'd finished puberty. Smile in public, sob in private, and make sure no one can read it on your face.

My extracurricular activity was work. I'd been clocking in somewhere since I turned fifteen, not because anyone forced me to, but because I understood the math of our situation. By junior year, when my mom retired on disability, it was clear enough: if I wanted anything past the basics, I'd have to earn it. A new pair of shoes, gas money, a movie ticket—all on me. It kept me busy and out of trouble.

At sixteen, I struck gold: a job at Media Play, in the music department. For anyone who didn't grow up in the late '90s or early 2000s, Media Play was the holy grail of entertainment escapism, a warehouse-sized mash-up of CDs, DVDs, posters, books, gadgets, and random pop-culture merchandise that made you feel cooler just by walking past it.

I picked up the language of sales fast. My favorite pitch was for the "Skip Dr.", a plastic contraption that promised to heal scratched discs. I'd hold it up, adjusting my voice as if I were letting someone in on a secret.

"Scratched CD? This'll save your album," I'd say, tilting it in my hand like a trick card.

They almost always nodded, hooked before they realized it. By the time we reached checkout, a spindle of blank CD-Rs had slipped into their basket too. "Just in case," I'd add, sealing the deal.

I thrived there. Adults didn't rattle me. A customer might come in annoyed—case broken, track skipping, humming a

half-remembered lyric. I'd step forward, steady and unbothered, and shift the entire mood. By the time they left, they had what they came for, and usually something they hadn't even known they wanted.

That confidence wasn't arrogance; it came from years of practice. It was muscle memory, built from years of handling emergencies most kids never saw. Making decisions in situations I had no business being part of, all before I was old enough to sit behind a steering wheel.

So when I was on the sales floor, it clicked. For once, there was structure. A system. And I clung to it, because everywhere else in my life felt like a fucking train wreck.

I turned seventeen while surgeons opened my mom's body again. This time it wasn't her lungs—it was her hip, or what remained of it. Years of Prednisone had kept her breathing, but it had also eaten her from the inside out. The drug puffed her face, packed over fifty pounds onto her petite frame, and disintegrated her right hip.

She needed a new hip, but the doctors had nowhere to go. If they kept her on Prednisone, there's a risk her bones would keep dissolving; if they took her off, her lungs would stop working. Every option led to a different kind of ending—they were just arguing over which came slower.

Because of the total hip replacement, her doctors stood at a crossroads with no good exits. Keep her on the steroid and watch her body break down piece by piece, or take her off it and risk her lungs collapsing. Neither choice promised survival, just different kinds of decline.

In the end, her pulmonologist made the call. They were switching her to an oral chemo agent—a new treatment plan with its own list of risks, but maybe, just maybe, a chance at slowing the damage without destroying everything else in the process.

THE BOYS REPUBLIC

Matters of the heart came with a different rulebook. My friends could scribble notes about crushes, turn red in the middle of math, and laugh it off at lunch. At their dinner tables, parents teased them gently, treating those blushes and confessions like a sweet, inevitable stage. Their feelings got eye rolls, ceremonial teasing, and maybe a smile that said, "You'll understand when you're older."

Their emotions had space. They could say them out loud, laugh about them, practice stumbling through the language of attraction without consequence. Mine had to stay—folded up and hidden like something I wasn't supposed to bring to school.

I sat cross-legged on my friend's bedroom floor, a half-eaten bag of chips between us, some action movie flickering in the background. The real entertainment was the debate—

who was the hottest girl in our class. Voices overlapped, each name thrown out louder than the last, one guy swearing up and down that the winner was a girl who still wore a retainer.

I laughed when the room expected me to, nodded along at the correct names. On the surface, I blended in, or at least that's what I told myself. But inside, something pulled tight. Not because I disagreed with them, but because I didn't belong in the conversation at all.

It's not that I didn't have feelings—I absolutely did. I just spent most of my energy hoping it wasn't apparent that I was staring at one of my friends, thinking, *whoever dates him is the luckiest girl alive.*

Hot. And also devastating.

When friends spilled all the details, from awkward hand-holding or first kisses, there was this energy—like they were being handed tiny keys to adulthood.

And I wanted that.

My crushes weren't bold. They lived quietly inside friendships and inside my head, settling into the background where no one would think to look. They revealed themselves in those blink-and-you-miss-it moments: a laugh we couldn't get through without doubling over, or a look that lingered just long enough for something to spark in me before I buried it.

In the moments that were ordinary to everyone else. The way his shoulder brushed mine in the backseat—crammed into our friend's car—lit my chest up like a fuse had been struck. I sat there, frozen, hyper-aware of every inch between us disappearing. Then I'd shift, casually, like nothing happened, even though something very much had.

My heart had already shattered a thousand private times before I ever made it to graduation. By the end of high school, I'd practically earned a PhD in unrequited love and emotional suppression. If there were letterman jackets for covertly longing for my straight friends, I'd have worn mine proudly—inside the same closet I couldn't come out of.

School became another thing slipping through my fingers. By junior year, I wasn't even pretending to keep up. Tests came back with bleeding corrections; whole sections were circled with comments I never read. My homework stayed buried at the bottom of my backpack, pressed into a greasy collage of cafeteria food and loose papers I'd stopped trying to organize.

On test days, I'd stare at a Scantron until the answer bubbles blurred together, shading them on autopilot. I'd scrawl my name across the top, the pencil dragging as if the simple act of claiming the assignment required more energy than I had. Then I'd watch the clock stretch every minute into something I had to endure instead of pass.

It wasn't apathy. My ADHD had a force of its own, and my brain was constantly bracing for whatever might go wrong next. It was hard to focus on quadratic equations when the place I slept felt closer to a medical triage zone than a home.

After junior year fell apart, I could see exactly where things were heading. Graduation was becoming a rumor. Every warning from teachers, every missed assignment, every test I'd half-assed had stacked into something I couldn't sidestep anymore. If I wanted any chance at pulling myself out of the hole I'd dug, something had to change.

Transferring schools felt like the closest thing to a reset. New hallways meant no one was waiting for the performance. A strict attendance policy was in place, so I couldn't skip class if I wanted to earn the credit. New teachers meant no old stories trailing behind me. And no friends pushing me towards trouble I couldn't afford.

In my head, it sounded clean: step into a new building, strip my life down to essentials, and rebuild from the ground up. Maybe in a place where no one already assumed they knew me, I could finally figure out how to show up for myself.

And then along came Daniel...

On the surface, we couldn't have looked more mismatched. Daniel carried New York in the way he moved—black Jordans that always seemed a little too clean, oversized jerseys that gave him the presence of someone twice his size, and this constant rhythm vibrating through his hands. His fingers never rested. They tapped against the desk with a confidence that suggested he was keeping time with a beat he only knew.

Whenever Sean Paul came on the radio, he lit up. His eyes went bright, and he'd start rapping every word under his breath, as if the track were his personal soundtrack and the rest of us were just lucky to overhear it.

I, meanwhile, was tuned to a completely different universe. My uniform was a rotation of Billabong hoodies, Abercrombie tees stretched from too many washes, and a beanie I treated like an extension of my body. Deftones, or Blindside, spilled through my headphones most days— loud, moody, and still somehow calmer than whatever was happening inside me.

Something in our contrast made space for a connection neither of us saw coming.

Daniel's laugh got to me first. It wasn't loud or attention-seeking, just this low, warm sound paired with a half-smile that felt aimed straight at me, and it stayed with me long after he looked away, the way a bass line sticks around after the song has already moved on.

I started chasing it—saying whatever I could to pull it out of him again. One stupid joke led to another, and before I realized what was happening, the two of us were trading jabs between classes, turning nothing conversations into something I looked forward to. What started as quick exchanges kept stretching, slipping into long riffs that made the rest of the day feel lighter.

That was the beginning: me trying to make him laugh, and him letting me.

We got close fast. On the surface, we still looked like opposites thrown together by a scheduling glitch, but from the start, there was something about Daniel that felt familiar in a way I didn't question until later. Most of our friends only saw the jokes and the energy between us; they never saw what sat underneath it.

We started from modest places, carrying the sort of history that could trap you if you let it. Both of us took more responsibility at home than anyone our age should've. His dad floated the edges of his life, just like mine. Daniel had two younger siblings who depended on him for everything from homework to helping keep the house running when his mom worked late. My role looked different, but came from the same place—I was the one watching my mom's health from the doorway, learning far too early how to step in when she couldn't.

At our core, beneath all the jokes and bravado, we were both just trying to climb out of the wreckage, and build something better from the debris.

Another October night settled around us, unhurried and wide open in a way we didn't question. My alarm clock kept flashing its numbers across the room, but neither of us bothered to look. We stayed on our backs, staring at the ceiling, letting the conversation wander wherever it wanted.

At one point, the room settled into a pause that didn't push for anything. It just existed and was big enough to hold both of us.

Then Daniel spoke.

"You've helped me more than anyone ever has."

It was dark, but I turned my head towards him — something in his voice had changed, coming from a place that rarely opened its mouth. And I waited for whatever was sitting behind that first sentence to show up.

"You actually believe in me," he said.

Nothing around us changed, yet I felt a sudden rush that made me aware of every inch of myself. Not in my chest exactly—lower, where things don't speak but still feel everything.

I went for a calm nod, something worthy of what he'd just given me. But I answered with a smile—that would've told the *whole* story in a well-lit room.

From that moment on, something in me rearranged itself.

At first, it happened in small ways—how I'd show up for him before he even hinted at needing anything, how I'd catch myself watching for his reactions before I made a decision.

He became the point around which everything in my day seemed to orbit. If he were in the room, my attention would follow. If he wasn't, I searched for him without meaning to. I told myself I was being a good friend—and I was, but beneath that, a mix of protectiveness, admiration, and something else I didn't dare examine too closely.

When he said my name, it felt like I was departing my body. His voice threaded itself through the most ordinary routines, caught me off guard when I was brushing my teeth or trying to fall asleep. Even hearing his name out loud felt loaded, almost fearful that my face exposed more than I intended to give away.

I convinced myself he needed me. That I understood him in a way no one else did, and maybe that meant I was supposed to hold the pieces he didn't know how to carry yet. It gave me purpose, something to rise to—but deep down, I knew what was really happening: I was bleeding out by the Band-Aid—a full-blown, big-ass codependent mess.

At seventeen, the gap between who I was and who I pretended to be grew wider by the week. The more I tried to stay who everyone thought I was, the more my authentic self faded into the background.

So I just existed, pretending not to notice how empty it all felt.

Daniel didn't see it.

He wasn't supposed to either, and he didn't do anything,

not really. That was the thing. He just existed—and that was enough to wreck every excuse I'd ever rehearsed. He never pretended otherwise.

My emotions felt too big for the space I had to hold them. The worst part wasn't wanting Daniel, even though that was terrifying. I didn't have a place to put those feelings.

Straight kids grow up learning the language of romance. They understand where to aim their hopes, who they're allowed to want, and how to read the signs. I didn't. I had skipped all the early milestones—puppy love, silly middle school attachments, the trial-and-error that teaches you how to live through it.

So when my first real attachment arrived, it didn't feel seventeen.

It felt younger. New in a way that made me feel behind and overwhelmed at the same time.

And because he was straight, and I was pretending to be, everything stayed one-sided, which made the whole experience stretch in opposite directions: too big for our friendship and impossible for anything more. But underneath all of that was the truth that I didn't know how to face:

I wanted something he could never give me.

And I didn't know how to let go of it.

By the time we noticed how distant we'd become, the break had already settled in. There was no slow fade. One day, we were inseparable; the next, we were two people pretending we didn't notice how far the other had drifted.

Losing him hurt. Yes, I missed him—just not in the "pass me a beer, bro" way our friendship box was built to contain.

My side of it came with extra wiring that didn't fit the script we were performing.

Daniel wasn't a crush. He wasn't a phase. He was the full-body "oh shit" I'd been trying not to acknowledge.

What cut deepest wasn't just the absence of him. It was everything he represented. He'd become the doorway to a part of myself that I wasn't brave enough to face...or allowed to reach for.

After that, nothing fit the way it used to.

I was hoping for a breakthrough—a moment with a girl where God would tap me on the shoulder and say, *There it is. You're good now.* So I "dated," if you can call it that. I told myself attraction was probably something you eased into, like jazz or vegetables.

But nothing stuck.

It messed with my head. I was staring at everything I was told I shouldn't want—and realizing I wanted it anyway. While also still pretending to like the brochure version of life that they kept handing out.

I was grieving someone I'd never be.

YOU CALLED ME THIS BEFORE I DID

A couple of months later. February settled in with its usual gloom—flat gray skies, cold that bit at anything exposed, the type of day that made you question why anyone lived in our state by choice. And before anyone from the Midwest rolls their eyes, yes, I was raised just north of Atlanta, where winter is basically a rumor. Still felt brutal.

I'd just walked out of class, one of those rooms with a door that opened straight into the parking lot, backpack sliding off one shoulder. I was tired, and I had to work that night.

Then I saw it.

At first, it barely registered, just a pale streak along the side of my car. Road dust, I told myself. Maybe someone swung

too hard when they'd opened the adjoining car's door. From a distance, it was nothing worth looking at twice.

But I stepped closer.

The cold hit my face, and something in me braced without knowing why. Another step, and the truth snapped into focus.

This wasn't dust.

And it wasn't a mistake.

Long, uneven gouges ran across the side of my blue '97 Acura Integra, deep enough to catch the light, crooked enough to know it was deliberate. My eyes followed the lines until they formed a word carved so hard into the paint that it looked engraved.

GAY.

All I could do was stand there, staring at a word I wasn't even saying to myself yet, etched into my car for anyone to read. The letters screamed: *We know. Even if you won't say it.* I had to drive a moving billboard announcing my deepest insecurity.

And I knew exactly who did it.

So did everyone else.

This kid, Phillip, made sure to claim his artwork—he told anyone who'd listen, retelling the story with that smug, performative grin he saved for moments he thought made him look tough.

And the security footage only made it worse.

The camera caught him walking toward my car—hood up, hands in his pockets, every step telegraphing intent. Then the frame jumped, almost politely, skipping over the exact moment it mattered. One second he was there, the next he was gone, the feed cutting out just long enough to protect him.

We didn't have the money to fix it. The damage was severe, but the car still moved when I turned the key. The engine didn't notice. The brakes still worked. On the inside, it was the same '97 Acura it had always been.

But I wasn't.

Driving it felt different. Walking up to it felt different. I sat behind the wheel of something that no longer felt like it belonged to me. A car that used to mean freedom now felt like a cell—a punishment I hadn't earned and deeply struggled with.

First came my friendship with Daniel—fracturing from the inside in a way I couldn't stop. Then the car. Two blows in quick succession, aimed at the softest parts of me. I didn't know how to fix what broke. And I wasn't about to workshop it in public.

Something in me finally snapped, and instead of exploding, I just folded inward. If emotions were going to keep misbehaving, I'd turn them off at the source.

There were perks to shutting down.

With nothing left to give socially, I redirected the whole mess into school. Homework suddenly had my full attention. Tests felt manageable. For the first time in years, I actually applied myself—and it worked. Straight A's and one B, the lone traitor I still refuse to forgive.

I sped through the rest of senior year. Graduated early. Picked up a full-time job. Filled out college applications like I was running a one-person assembly line. I stayed polished. Productive. Unreachable—the holy trinity of "don't ask me how I'm doing."

My logic was simple: if I kept every hour packed, no one would slow down long enough to ask fundamental questions. And if they didn't ask…

…I didn't have to answer.

Control became my drug of choice. Not because I was naturally disciplined, but because everything else felt hijacked. My body, my friendships, my voice. While there were perks that came with my newly discovered yearn for perfection, there was also a dark side.

Because beneath all that "discipline," I'd started to see food—especially meat—as a threat. I took control of the one thing that felt mine fully: my plate. I needed proof I could commit to and control something, even if I had no idea what the price would be.

When asked why, I recited all the right lines, clean, rehearsed, and borrowed from someone else's convictions. But it was not for health, not for ethics. It was all for control.

Then I became obsessed with losing weight.

Before the weight loss, I spent most of my time trying to hide behind my clothes and my personality. Taking my shirt off wasn't even on the menu. That got shut down back in fifth grade when my friend Lola announced, in PE, that my boobs were bigger than hers. From that moment on, I treated my torso like a classified secret.

Back in October of my senior year, I looked…well-fed. Let's call it that. In photos, I had the round, cheerful face people swear is "adorable," which is code for: *your body arrives three seconds before you do.* I could feel myself jiggle when I jogged, bent over, or just existed.

In five months, I dropped from that soft, 170-pound version of myself to someone who had to cinch his belt to the last hole just to keep his jeans from sliding off. Then it showed up in the mirror: my face losing its usual fullness, my collarbones starting to announce themselves, my clothes hanging in ways they'd never done before. Week after week, the kid I'd been was disappearing, until nearly fifty pounds were gone.

I started "eating" once a day, if you could call it eating. Most days, I picked at food like it might bite me back. A granola bar. Half a sandwich. A milkshake. Whatever felt small enough not to undo the progress. I'd drink water until my stomach stretched sufficiently to feel full.

By spring, people treated me differently without even realizing it. Eyes lingered in ways I'd never experienced before. Compliments came from teachers, friends, girls, coworkers— "You look great"—as if I'd unlocked some prestigious achievement instead of severely restricting my caloric intake in an obsessive manner.

I soaked it in, not because I was hunting for compliments, but it felt good because it finally gave me proof that all the restrictions, all the rules, skipped meals, all my rituals had been worth something. They all added up to something I could finally point to and say: *this, at least, is mine to manage.*

Even when it was unhealthy.

And honestly, starving myself still felt safer than being gay.

SHE ALMOST NEVER KNEW ME

I didn't come out because I was ready. I came out because life has a way of shoving you forward, whether you've caught your breath or not.

It was February 2005. I was nineteen, still clinging to the scaffolding of who I thought I was supposed to be, just months away from my twenties. That's the intersection where the illusion finally gave out. Not a dramatic shatter—it started as a tiny hit. And once it cracked, everything began to give way.

For a while, it looked like we'd finally caught a break. Three and a half years went by without sirens, without scrubs at the door, without me memorizing the layout of an ICU room. The house stopped feeling like a trauma center. The oxygen tanks stayed in the corner, and my mom's lung disease backed off enough for us to pretend that it might stay that way. Life didn't feel borrowed; it felt like we'd finally stepped into the version we were always meant to have.

My mom threw herself back into life, cooking full spreads on random weeknights, because she could. She started saying yes to dinners out, yes to dancing with her friends, yes to anything that made her feel rooted in the world again. You never would have guessed anyone had ever whispered the word "sick" around her.

She even started sewing again; it became a full-on side hustle, turning the dining room table into a fabric jungle—curtain panels draped over chairs, patterns stacked on side tables, spools of thread in every drawer. Mom had clients—real ones. Projects on the calendar, measurements jotted down in a spiral notebook, and a sparkle in her eye I hadn't seen in years.

I designed her business cards myself: "Sew Precise", printed in a bold serif font that, in her words, looked "professional and with heart."

The sewing machine started with a quick surge, then slowed as she eased off the pedal—rising and falling in uneven waves. It reminded me of the sound of the ventilator: mechanical, steady, and with breath behind it. Only this time, it wasn't keeping someone alive; it was building something.

It's strange how two opposites can run side by side—hope and hiding, ease and editing yourself. I was finally catching a break, but still looking over my shoulder.

My mom was in the middle of the biggest comeback that no one had ever heard of. Meanwhile, I was knee-deep in my own personal "Don't Ask, Don't Tell," starring as both the lead and the secret.

Still, I kept trying to wedge myself into the version of life I thought I was supposed to want—a wife, two kids, maybe a golden retriever named something respectable like Ted. I pictured myself as the dad who stood quietly in the doorway at night, just to make sure everything was okay.

That version of me felt noble. Familiar. Safe.

But it wasn't real.

I had to let him go because he was never mine to begin with. I wasn't building a future. I was rehearsing a role I thought might make the rest of my life easier to explain.

On paper, I looked steady enough—working full-time at a clothing store, keeping my GPA high enough to hold onto my scholarship. From the outside, I seemed balanced, ambitious, even put together. The real burnout came from pretending.

For nearly three years, I'd been controlling food, my way of convincing myself I had at least one part of my life handled. I kept my weight at 125 or below—that number became a boundary I couldn't cross. Then my skin changed. I'd never struggled with breakouts, but that year, angry cysts surfaced along my jaw, across my torso, down my back. In retrospect, it was my body that was speaking on my behalf, pushing truths outward before I could gather the courage to say any of them myself.

The anxiety of someone asking the wrong question or noticing something I didn't hide well enough wore me down until the version of me everyone expected slipped out of reach. I'd pulled inward before, back in eighth grade, and when things with Daniel blew up, but this time the retreat tightened around my throat like a reticulated python.

One-on-one conversations became the hardest. It felt like being pinned to a microscope slide—held in place, every flaw lit up under scrutiny. You could see the fractures, the parts that didn't quite belong, the effort it took to seem normal. The more I tried to blend in, the more unsteady I felt. I missed the ease I used to have, the spark that made me feel connected to people instead of alienated from them.

One Sunday, my colleague Chelsea and I stepped out to grab Starbucks for the team. On the walk there, I kept scanning the sidewalk, hoping we'd bump into someone—anyone—who could fold into our path. A third person meant safer territory, fewer direct questions, fewer chances for the conversation to turn toward me. Two people made everything feel too exposed. I needed the buffer.

At the top of the stairs outside Starbucks, she slowed. Her hand brushed the rail, more to steady the moment than herself. "I want to ask you something," she said, choosing each word with care, as if she were opening a box she wasn't sure she had permission to touch. "This is coming from a good place. I just...I feel like there's something you're not saying. And it feels sad. People care about you. That wouldn't change."

I kept my eyes on the concrete, watching her sentences settle at our feet. None of them felt accidental.

"I can't talk to you about this right now," I said, the only boundary I dared to draw. I didn't wait for her response. I yanked open the Starbucks door and made a beeline for the counter.

After conversations like that, I'd unravel for days—sometimes weeks. I'd move through rooms on high alert,

scanning faces too long, dissecting glances, tone shifts, whispers. Watching how people looked at me when they thought I wasn't looking.

Was that what everyone talked about the second I left the room?

I didn't need another well-intended reminder that they'd "love me no matter what." If anything, those lines made me pull back harder. If you cared about me, you'd stop pushing—because you'd notice how much it shook me. I didn't need soft voices or gentle nudges. I needed space.

If I was going to share this part of myself, it had to be on my terms. Their validation didn't comfort—it crowded.

If. When. If.

It wasn't that I rejected their kindness. I just couldn't hold it. You can't absorb love you don't think you deserve.

That night, I headed straight for my room, ready to shut down and disappear. But halfway down the hall, I stopped.

A cough.

Not a casual throat-clear or seasonal tickle, this one came from somewhere deeper, somewhere she hadn't had to reach in a long time. And just like that, it was back. No warning. No warm-up. Just picking up where it left off—louder, faster, meaner.

Two days earlier, Mom had been in the living room folding laundry, bragging about her new workout DVD and how it was "no joke." Now she couldn't finish a sentence without stopping to catch her breath.

And on February 8, the bomb went off.

Her lips were turning blue.

It felt like 1999 all over again. Or 2001. The panic never cared which year it was—it showed up the same every time. You'd think after repeatedly seeing this scene throughout my childhood, I'd know how to steady myself better, but my voice still broke as I tried to give the operator our address.

The sirens rose in the distance, building until the driveway answered with the crunch of tires. Doors slammed. Red light spilled through the windows and swept across the walls in steady beats, creating a pattern I'd learned long before this night. I stayed where I was, listening. I didn't need to look outside to understand what came next.

My mom had spent years rebuilding—piece by piece. And in an instant, that progress gave way, and I couldn't stop a single inch of it.

She lay unconscious in the ICU, motionless under a maze of tubes and monitors. The machines did the work her lungs couldn't manage.

I sat there gripping the edge of her bed, and all I could think was:

If she dies tonight, she'll never really know me.

The real one. The full one.

Only the version she thought she knew.

LETTERS

In that ICU room, something within me broke loose. Not neatly. Not quietly. But in a way that made it clear there was no going back.

My mom was everything. She showed up for every school event, every scraped knee, every late-night panic. Her lungs failed her. Her joints ached. Some days, just walking to the mailbox knocked the breath out of her. And still—on my birthday—she'd hang streamers, light candles, hum the tune while cutting a cake she made. At dinner, she'd plate everything with care, like presentation could hold the day together.

I had watched her body endure storms most people couldn't imagine, seen her spirit stagger beneath burdens that would have broken others. And still, some part of me believed that I, not the illness, might be the thing that finished her.

That the moment I laid down my truth, it would strike her harder than any diagnosis ever had.

But the lying—dodging questions, changing the subject, pretending—all it had done was build a cage so elaborate that I mistook it for a home. I'd been living two lives in one skin, and the seams were starting to tear apart.

Mom left the hospital nineteen days later. The discharge papers were barely signed before my life split into three shifts. I'd finish work or a full day of classes, then head straight into her aftercare as if I'd secretly earned a medical degree.

I knew the routine well and moved through it without hesitation: sorting medications, setting up her breathing treatments, keeping the house running, checking on her through the night—then waking up the next morning to finish studying to keep my scholarship afloat.

My mind never went quiet. It felt crowded, layers of worry, responsibility, guilt, and fear all running at once, and each one pulled at me in its own direction. There was no clear place to set any of it down. No prayer, no pep talk, no late-night deal I tried to make with myself could slow it. Everywhere I went, that noise came along. If it had legs, it would've out-walked me, waving from ten steps ahead like, "Hurry up."

Nights stretched on forever. I'd end up flat on my back, staring at the ceiling fan, listening to the white noise of my mom's oxygen machine down the hall. I'd walk myself through pleasant thoughts, which included hits such as: What if her breathing stops before morning? What if I never sort myself out? What if the people I love can't meet me where I

am once they know the whole truth? *Would I ever get to have a family of my own, or was that another thing I'd have to bury?*

I couldn't tell where one ended and the next began. Son. Brother. Christian. Friend. Student. Some days it felt like I was failing all of them at once.

School was the first thing to give. I cut my course load in half at Kennesaw State, hoping it would buy me enough breathing room to keep everything else from toppling. The fear of tanking my GPA sat in the front of my mind, because that scholarship was the only reason the whole operation stayed upright.

I wasn't ready to come out. Not even in theory. The idea circled my mind for years, making appearances during late-night spirals, but vanishing the second daylight hit. I kept telling myself I'd get there eventually, but "eventually" stayed far away.

Then, mom almost died, and "eventually" turned into right now.

She'd earned the truth. She'd fought too hard to leave without knowing me. Keeping quiet would be louder in my life than anything grief could bring.

I still couldn't say it. Even alone, I'd stand in front of the mirror and barely force out, *I'm gay.* Every time I tried, I felt like a stand-in reciting another person's truth.

A face-to-face confession wasn't going to happen, so I ended up writing a letter.

Not because it felt courageous, or tidy, or poetic. It was just the only way the truth stood a chance of making it out without breaking me in the process.

I sat at my desk and wrote until the page felt crowded. I told her how much I loved her, how worn thin I felt from hiding in plain sight, how this wasn't confusion or rebellion or anything that could be prayed away.

I explained that I hadn't chosen any of it. This part of me had been there since the beginning, placed in me with the same intention as every other part of who I was. It wasn't a detour, and then I wrote the most challenging part: I'd held this secret on my own for years, and I'd run out of room to keep it buried.

Then I folded the letter, left it on the counter, and waited.

And waited.

And waited.

When we finally met face-to-face, she looked at me, eyes already wet.

Not with rage. It wasn't disgust...but something closer to heartbreak. I felt her mourning me in real time, even though I was still sitting right there.

She told me she loved me—unconditionally. I believed her. But it wasn't that simple. It came tangled in qualifiers, in pauses.

Then came the worries, just stacked gently in front of me. The world could be unkind. People could be cruel. And beneath that, the fear that she'd somehow caused this, or that my dad's absence had been too loud, or that not having a steady male presence had influenced something in me.

None of it matched the truth, but I could see the concern sitting behind her questions. Her heart was in the right place; that part I never questioned. She was trying to protect me and make sense of it the only way she knew how.

But once the words were out—my truth on the table—there was no rewinding it. No pretending this conversation hadn't happened. No pushing it back into the dark.

My mom never opened the door to that conversation—not then, not later. That part stayed untouched. Still, her love never dimmed. Nothing about the way she held me in her life changed; no cold shoulder, no slow retreat.

What did change was the space around the topic itself. Mom kept it at arm's length, as though naming it would lock it into permanence. Her avoidance wasn't cruel—it was cautious, a kind of emotional detour she hoped I'd walk with her.

It wasn't simple.

Offering her grace meant biting down on my own hurting and admitting I was still finding my footing with it, too. I wanted understanding from her, but I hadn't even entirely given that to myself yet.

She'd grown up in the South long before my version of it. I thought it was tough in my generation—cartoonish stereotypes on TV, youth pastors "warning us", classmates whispering slurs behind lockers. Hers was an entirely different landscape.

For her, homosexuality wasn't ever discussed. If it did, it showed up in hushed conversations, in headlines that framed it as a problem to solve or a danger to avoid. So, when I came out, she wasn't reacting to me, not really. She was responding to every story she'd ever absorbed, every stereotype repeated over kitchen tables.

That was the script she had. And suddenly, her child had stepped into the center of it.

Even in the mid-2000s, being gay wasn't something most people announced and celebrated. It still lived in sideways comments, in rumors traded between friends, in message boards picking apart a celebrity's haircut as "evidence." Public visibility wasn't brand partnership or parades; it was a grainy paparazzi photo followed by a stiff "no comment" from a publicist.

That was the landscape—curiosity, denial, and an underlying discomfort everyone pretended not to notice. And 2005 carried its own energy. It felt like the country was still recovering from Massachusetts opening the door to gay marriage the year before.

The national debate framed homosexuality as a moral collapse, a direct threat to "family values," with conversion therapy paraded as an easy solution. Where I lived—in the South—it was worse. It was a spiritual emergency.

For someone like me, a gay Christian, the message was suffocatingly clear: faith and sexuality weren't presented as two parts of a whole person. They were treated as opponents, impossible to hold at the same time. It was a trip walking past the "God Hates Fags" group in the free-speech zone at college. They were convinced they were talking about people who were far from God, and there I was, gay as ever, walking by with Flyleaf, a Christian hard rock band, blasting on my iPod.

I knew my heart. I knew I wasn't immoral.

But the truth is, I barely understood what being gay even meant. I kept that part of myself sealed off, tucked so far behind everything else that it felt borrowed from another lifetime. I only knew it was something I wasn't supposed to touch.

When you've spent years training yourself to hide, honesty doesn't burst through the door; it needs an excavator. By the end, the whole emotional setup looks straight out of an episode of *Hoarders*. Old beliefs stacked on top of insecurities, shame wedged under the couch, irrational guilt leaning against the doorway, and a narrow pathway carved between piles of things you never dealt with.

Then comes staying in its presence, without turning my face toward anything easier than honesty.

For so long, I thought honesty would cost me my faith. At least that's what it always felt like, anyway—that being gay meant stepping away from God. When the truth about who I was finally pushed its way to the open, I always prepared myself for a spiritual fallout.

But something surprising happened instead.

Christ didn't move.

People had always warned me about God's supposed reaction—anger, disappointment. They described Him in a way that didn't match the voice I'd grown up praying to. Their version of Christ sounded irritated, fear-based. Mine sounded steady. Patient. The same presence that sat with me during hospital nights, panic, and every version of loneliness I'd collected since childhood.

So part of this whole process—this excavation meant sorting through what Christ actually said and what other people decided he must've meant. I had a lot of work ahead, but I realized something simple:

If Christ wanted distance from me, I would've felt it long before I ever admitted I was gay.

In movies, coming out is a full production—cue tears, applause, someone storming off. My coming out felt more like renewing a driver's license. A few awkward steps, some paperwork, a photo I hated—and then it was done. I suppose details don't matter, because I did it. I'd said it. And thankfully, I'd never have to come out to her again.

After I came out, it felt like stepping out of one box just meant stepping into another—one that told me how I was supposed to act, talk, dress, and think.

Another performance.

Another role to rehearse.

I never wanted to be reduced to a talking point. The last thing I wanted was to turn into a stereotype people used to prove how open-minded they weren't. I didn't want my life to become a measuring stick for someone else's intolerance.

What scared me most was the idea of my sexuality becoming the headline that swallowed everything else. I had humor, faith, ambition, trauma, opinions, flaws, kindness, stubbornness—entire worlds inside me—and I didn't want all of it flattened into a single label.

I just wanted to be Trey. Not Trey on defense. Not Trey-in-pieces.

The whole me.

TINY HIDDEN BOMBS

Two years after coming out to my mom, I was living on my own in Atlanta, more than 175 miles north of her new home in South Georgia. She had moved there in 2006 to be closer to my sister, while I carved out my independence in the city.

That afternoon, I was at my desk, surrounded by stacks of flashcards, half-empty coffee cups, and my Spanish notes from Professor Hance—one of my favorite professors who made even the hardest lessons into something I looked forward to. I was mid-sentence in a verb chart when my phone vibrated.

Mom.

The moment I answered, I noticed it. Her voice carried less of its usual warmth, stretched thinner, almost brittle. Before I could ask anything, she rushed with "Trey, don't worry, I'm not hospital-sick," a relapse of her lung disease, BOOP.

Then she mentioned the migraines that had been bothering her for weeks.

"Things look blurry sometimes," she confessed, almost offhand, but I caught the concern behind her words. She described seeing doubles—objects sliding on top of each other until the room seemed off-balance, especially when she turned her head too fast or in the wrong direction.

She brushed it off quickly, her voice firm, almost rehearsed. "Don't worry. I'm not putting this off. I've got an MRI in a few days."

I repeated her words in my head until they felt like fact. She was fine. She had to be fine, even though I now had a death grip on my phone.

When my mom called with the MRI results a few days later, I was in the kitchen, watching the microwave clock tick down. I couldn't even remember what I'd put inside.

"Two aneurysms," she said. Just two words—and the whole world stopped.

Two silent bombs tucked away inside her skull, waiting to detonate.

I froze. The microwave beeped, prolonged and incessant, but I didn't move to open it. The food, whatever it was, didn't matter. All I could hear were those two words, circling, rewriting everything I thought was ordinary about that afternoon.

My mom's brain surgery was scheduled right in the middle of my midterms. She insisted I sit for my exams first.

"Finish strong," she told me. "Then drive to Athens Regional. There's nothing you can do for me that day anyway."

She reminded me of how far I'd already come—how hard I'd fought to get into college, how lucky I was to have an academic scholarship. She wanted me to see the bigger picture, the life I was building beyond that week.

But sitting in those classrooms, flipping through textbooks, I felt like I was pretending. Words on the page blurred into nothing. I wasn't in class. I was already in Athens, pacing sterile hospital corridors in my head, listening for news that could change everything.

When the exams were over, I packed my car and pointed it toward Athens. The drive felt suspended in time, like a sentence cut off mid-thought—nothing but a highway full of what-ifs.

All I knew, truly knew for sure, was that she had made it through surgery. She was alive. Stable. That word—stable— was all I had to hold onto.

Mile by mile, the abstract turned concrete. The closer I came, the more it sank in: this wasn't another routine stay, not the kind I'd grown used to over nine hospital visits. This was different.

This wasn't another pulmonary flare I could recite in my sleep, or a hip replacement I'd already mapped out in memory. I knew those corridors, those routines.

This was different.

This was her skull.

Her brain.

Open cranial surgery.

Bone saws.

Clamps biting down on blood vessels thinner than a thread.

Surgeons can cut with precision and stitch with perfection, yet what wakes up on the other side might not look anything like the person who went under. Even when everything goes "right," recovery from brain surgery is never uniform. It's a gamble every single time. Maybe her memory would still be there. Maybe her voice.

Or maybe the part of her that made her, her, would come back altered, dimmed, or not at all.

When I first saw her after surgery, she looked smaller. Not in size, but in spirit, like the operation had pressed her into a quieter, more fragile version of herself. In those first days, her voice was scarce. When mom spoke, the words came out thinner and more hesitant, as if she were testing them before committing.

A broad white bandage circled her head, covering the place where surgeons had peeled back to the bone. On the table beside her sat the things I'd brought—dry shampoo she'd need for weeks, since washing her hair wasn't an option, and the things the nurses had left: Sudoku puzzles and flashcards, tools to stimulate parts of her brain that might have been disrupted.

Even though the procedure went well, her surgeon didn't sugarcoat anything. He suspected a mini-stroke had happened on the table, and no one could say how much of her baseline would return. It could take weeks, maybe months, before we'd know the full cost.

The changes surfaced fast. She stumbled on things so simple it stopped me cold—my birthday, the names of our dogs. Sometimes the answer arrived after a long pause in searching. Other times, the thought just drifted away before it ever formed.

Even her handwriting was different. What used to be bold and fluid had shrunk into cramped, uneven letters, a script that seemed almost apologetic, as if she no longer felt entitled to take up space.

What unsettled me most wasn't what she said; it was what she couldn't say anymore. Tears wouldn't come. Laughter wouldn't surface. She later told a psychiatrist she felt emotionally dead, a jarring admission from the woman who used to tear up over a Hallmark commercial before the music even swelled.

For the first time in my life, I couldn't reach her. Our usual shortcut to connection, jokes, shared humor, the quick spark of "you get me", had vanished. Sitting there beside her, I could feel the distance stretching out, and I had no idea how to close it.

A ROOM I'D BEEN BUILDING MY WHOLE LIFE

Before I could spell my own name, I'd already learned how to hold an audience. My body hit its marks, but some part of me hovered outside of the performance, watching the whole thing play out. The small distance turned into a skill; it taught me how to read a room before the room even knew I was paying attention.

What steadied me was laughter, not just mine, but theirs. Watching someone's shoulders loosen, or their eyes glimmer after a joke, always soothed something in me, too. Even when no one realized it, they were always my audience.

A year after my mom's brain surgery, I was stumbling through the senior year of college, mainly running on coffee and nerves. I managed the café at a bookstore—authority on paper. Still, in practice, it meant scrubbing dried chai off

counters and explaining the difference between a latte and a cappuccino to people who didn't care.

Facebook was still the dominant platform back then, and we turned retail survival into a digital documentary. As a team, we were like feral animals. Katie, Meghan, and I turned slow shifts into theater, pranks, and performance art that no customer asked for.

Henry the Cat, the café's plush mascot, became our favorite victim. Some days, he was staged mid-pelvic thrust against a bag of beans. On other days, he was stuffed into the sandwich case, shrink-wrapped between turkey clubs, grinning out at confused customers.

When Octo-Mom, a California woman who gave birth to eight babies at once and became instant tabloid fuel, dominated headlines, I grabbed a marker and drew her face on our promo sign. Our big push was a blackberry crème latte, and I thought, *Why not?*

The result was a lopsided portrait with overdrawn lips, uneven eyes, and a stare...but it worked. Underneath, I scribbled: "Blackberry Crème Latte. Try one, or eight!" It was so ridiculous that customers actually stopped, pointed, and laughed. Management wanted sales; I gave them a tabloid parody on the café blackboard.

Sometimes I showed up in safety goggles over my glasses, dead serious, serving lattes as if eye protection was part of the uniform. No one questioned it; they'd just nod, occasionally tip, and walk away, while I kept a straight face.

We'd plant fake "customer shopping lists" around the

store, and lurk nearby, waiting for someone to take the bait. One of my favorites read:

Is It Rejection, or Did I Imagine The Entire Relationship
Bible (King James Edition)
Big Boobs, Little Budget.

The handwriting was messy enough to look authentic, the kind of note you'd imagine falling out of a purse or pocket. Watching customers stumble across one and squint at the titles was its own kind of theatre.

Then came *the* photo.

One poorly timed upload.

One click.

One coworker who enforced store policy like she was auditioning for *Cops: Barista Unit.*

I'd taken it myself, snapped while shelving books across the aisle. The woman stood there in shiny navy leggings, thick white socks bunched halfway up her calves, and bright red clogs that looked like they belonged in a costume trunk. I couldn't resist. I posted it on Facebook with the caption: *"What not to wear."*

At the time, it felt harmless, just another entry in our running series of ridiculousness—right next to Henry Cat wrapped in plastic wrap in the pastry case.

Instead, fired.

Turns out, corporate wasn't all that thrilled about employees posting candid customer photos. Something about a "zero tolerance" policy and "invasion of privacy"—which, honestly, felt dramatic.

At that point in my life, it turned out to be the best thing that could have happened to me.

I was twenty-four, unemployed for the first time since fifteen. Then I finally did the thing I'd been talking about for years: I signed up for a stand-up open mic.

The Laughing Skull Lounge sat buried in Midtown, easy to miss unless someone pointed you toward it. Hidden behind The Vortex Bar & Grill, it felt less like a club and more like a secret handshake. New comics dotted the room, eyes glued to napkins, whispering punchlines to themselves like they were cramming for a final. But I wasn't anxious. I was ready.

Marshall Chiles: the owner, emcee, and gatekeeper of the stage—stood behind the mic, scanning the crowd with the easy authority of a man who'd lived a thousand nights under the lights.

His silver hair caught the glow, giving him that "silver fox" polish that made him look equal parts professor and showman. The collar of his crisp shirt framed his face, a detail that set him apart from the comics in jeans and hoodies waiting their turn. He squinted into the back of the room, pausing just long enough to build tension. Then he said my name.

I stood, stepped forward, and the instant my foot hit the stage, it was like flipping a breaker. Behind me, the backdrop glowed in deep red panels, throwing everything into high contrast. My hair was styled into its trademark spike, black shirt hugging close, white belt popping against faded wash bootcut jeans.

No overthinking, no mental gymnastics—just me, the mic, and a rhythm I didn't know was wired into me. I'll never forget the opening lines of that set:

"Because of my hair, people tell me I look like a mix of Jimmy Neutron and Samantha Ronson—Lindsay Lohan's lesbian DJ girlfriend. Or a bargain-bin version of Adam Levine."

The room erupted.

A sold-out crowd, their laughter crashing against me. That sound hit my bloodstream and set every nerve on fire. I'd been chasing that feeling my entire lifetime. It turned me on in the purest sense, body alive, begging me to keep going.

I was riding the moment, completely unplanned. Thirty seconds in, under the lights, the words slipped out—and they would change my life forever.

"So, I'm a vegetarian—which obviously means I don't eat...pussy.

"But you probably figured that out from how much hair product I use."

I hadn't planned on talking about being gay—certainly not in front of a crowd. On paper, I'd been out for four years. A few friends knew. My mom and sister knew. But standing there, mic in hand, spotlight pinning me in place, it felt different.

Strangely, I felt safer on that stage—safer with a room full of strangers and familiar faces watching—than I ever had in private. And the world didn't crack open or spit me out. It laughed with me.

For the first time, I didn't tuck it inside parentheses or soften it into an apology. That feeling—the one that used to shrink me in locker rooms and classrooms, that used to make me triple check my tone, the way my hands moved, the way I simply existed—lost its grip that night.

From there, the jokes tumbled out one after another, the crowd still laughing at one line while my mind was already three steps ahead, riffing, twisting, chasing tangents, then snapping back just in time for the punchline to land.

And I walked offstage taller than I walked on.

As the crowd thinned and the last laughs soaked into the walls of the Laughing Skull, Marshall waved me over.

No grin. No empty "good set." Just a long look. Then, finally:

"That was something," he said. Then, after a beat:

"Was it really your first time?"

Coming from a man who'd watched hundreds of comics bomb, burn, or barely scrape by—it felt less pat on the back, more a marker in the ground.

I'd never felt gifted. Never effortless. Just grinding at things that came easily to everyone else. I spent years ricocheting off every structure handed to me. Team sports were a disaster— I've got the hand-eye coordination of someone six tequila shots deep. Classrooms? ADHD made every one of them feel like an Ironman event while sitting still.

This fit.

And the best part? Marshall saw it, too.

"Come back Saturday," he said. No small talk. No "maybe". Just that, a door. Open.

After that, life turned up. My last six months in college were a mash-up of lectures, open mics, and sneaking in punchline tweaks mid-conversation with anyone who stood still long enough. I was also balancing a production internship at Turner Broadcasting's Adult Swim—a fever dream for anyone who grew up on weird cartoons and weirder timing.

A few months after graduation, Marshall offered me a full-time job at the Laughing Skull.

This wasn't a "Congrats, kid, I'm throwing you a bone" moment. Marshall ran the place like a comedy dojo crossed with a Navy SEAL training camp. No slackers. No fluff. He was part club owner, part comedy sommelier—only interested in the bold stuff with real notes of wit.

He didn't care who you were, rookie, veteran, gay, straight, neurotic, barely holding it together. If you were smart and showed up ready, you had a place. His vision was to build an incubator for clever, fearless comedy.

By day, I was basically the club's one-man marketing department, stationed in the back with a folding chair and a laptop that ran so hot it could toast an everything bagel. I cranked out flyers, managed social media, and dove into "growth marketing"—a term that, at the time, sounded like a pyramid scheme.

Most afternoons, I'd sneak into nearby hotels and slip our promo cards into concierge racks with all the confidence of a clearance-rack James Bond. If I had extra time, I'd plaster QR codes in bar bathrooms, between the graffiti and inspirational quotes.

Off-stage, I worked as a producer and part-time emotional triage nurse. I pieced together last-minute schedules, talked comics down from existential ledges, and hunted down regional acts that could crush without killing the weird brilliance that made the Skull what it was.

Working for Marshall felt like I'd finally caught the current I'd been chasing without knowing I was even in the water. It changed everything for me, and it was the most alive I'd felt in years.

I was hooked. All-in. If Atlanta had a heartbeat, I was synced to it, pounding seven nights a week with no breaks and no Plan B. I'd hit any stage that would take me—sometimes three or four a night—grimy backrooms with shaky stools. One pizza joint where the mic died every third word and the bartender heckled like it was part of the set. And of course, The Laughing Skull.

It didn't matter.

The rush lived in the unknown—walking into a room, tossing out a half-formed bit just to see if it could stand. The dead air, the stray laugh, the creative spark you didn't plan. Learning to work the crowd, bend with them, and build something in real time.

One week, I was testing a concept about QuestChat—the late-night dating hotline where women in five-inch heels and spray-on tops lounged across leather sectionals, moaning into landlines like that's just how they passed the time.

They all looked suspiciously available and aggressively bored, tossing out lines like, "Looking for hot local singles... just like you," flirtatiously inviting the kind of guy who thought calling a stranger to breathe heavily into a receiver was a real shot at love.

The following week, I was on a soundstage shooting a pilot with Atlanta legends Drivin' N' Cryin'. I even pulled in my friend, a talented comic named Sarah Cooper, before she went viral for turning lip-syncing into political performance art.

The storm finally eased. No late-night emergencies. No mental math about oxygen levels or whether we were one cough away from another ambulance ride. I wasn't bracing for impact or keeping a secret that could destroy my world.

I was gliding. I was using the one thing I knew without question God had given me: the ability to make people laugh. It didn't fix everything, but it woke something up. Something that had been waiting. For the first time in my twenties, I wasn't white-knuckling my way through life. I was in it entirely, freely—and it felt damn good.

WELCOME TO THE CLERMONT LOUNGE

Atlanta served up one of its signature afternoons—humid, bloated, and determined to make every pore regret being open. My friend Erin and I had just wrapped up a brunch so boozy it probably qualified as a wellness retreat, if your metric for wellness was belly laughs and three pitchers of mimosas.

Naturally, we decided the next stop was the Atlanta Zoo. Still tipsy and fully committed to whatever came next, we wandered the exhibits like escaped camp counselors and snapped selfies with flamingos. Photobombed goats. Giggled through existential debates in front of the otters. Pure unfiltered joy, only bottomless drinks and zero responsibilities can produce.

We were strutting back, buzzed, sun-dazed, and high

on our own hilarity—when my phone buzzed—unknown California number.

I glanced at it, expecting spam or a *You Could Be Debt-Free!* Instead, a text:

Hey, Trey—it's Margaret Cho. Marshall said you're running the shows at the Laughing Skull. I'm in town over the summer...

I froze.

Erin kept talking about a llama we'd allegedly overfed, "Wait—what's wrong?"

I didn't say a word. Just turned the phone toward Erin, arms raised as if I was presenting a rare artifact.

She gasped. I nodded. The mimosas had prepared us for many things. This was not one of them.

Margaret. Fucking. Cho is texting me.

I'd met Margaret the year before at the inaugural Laughing Skull Comedy Festival. It was one of those backstage collisions that doesn't announce itself as anything special, but the moment she spoke, there was something grounding about the way she carried herself. She had a steadiness that stood out in a place full of anxious energy and inflated egos. It wasn't friendship yet—not even close. But I walked out of that festival thinking, *I hope our paths cross again.*

Honestly, I never expected her to remember me. I wasn't even sure I said anything memorable. There's also a decent chance I blacked out mid-sentence and nodded through the rest.

Margaret was in town filming the television show, *Drop Dead Diva*, and the Laughing Skull turned into her home

base while she worked out material for her next tour, *Cho Dependent*. Before long, she wasn't just a regular in the green room; she was a regular in my life.

Watching Margaret work out material was like sneaking into a lab where a mad genius made truth explosive. No preamble. No polish. Just raw fire and fearless honesty, hammering each line until it hit like a freight train. She wasn't testing jokes so much as she was dragging them, bloody and breathing, into existence.

She took me under her wing, but not in that "let me teach you, young grasshopper" kind of way. It was casual. Natural. We hung out a lot. Sometimes post-show, sometimes over dinner, sometimes just trading stories that ping-ponged from ridiculous to gut-wrenching in under five minutes.

She'd squeezed into the spot beside me on that battered greenroom couch and draped her arm around the back cushion. Her confidence was effortless, threaded through everything from the bold stretch of ink running across her upper arm to the flash of a bright scarf knotted at her neck. Margaret looked like the color in a room that had given up on it.

The lighting inside that back room wasn't kind to anyone, but somehow it suited her—warm on her face, catching the edge of her grin as she sized me up.

"You don't write like most people," she told me, leaning in with that knowing look she had. "You write onstage. Your set shifts with you. It feels alive—like you're sculpting it as it comes to you."

That comment hit me in a way she probably didn't intend. Her matter-of-fact delivery made the room feel like a shoebox.

She wasn't flattering me. She was diagnosing me. And she wasn't wrong.

She'd named something I'd always assumed only I could feel: the way my mind ran ten beats ahead of my mouth, dragging the set with it. Less blueprint, more jazz. My ADHD takes the wheel, gleeful and unbothered. One offhand comment from the crowd? I'd spin off into a tangent about the absurdity of gendered shampoo or the universe of nightmare customers. None of it existed on paper. None of it *could* exist on paper.

None of that magic shows up if I'm chained to a desk.

"See?" she added, nudging me with her shoulder, "That's your thing. Don't tame it."

That night, she gave me language for something I'd been doing my whole life without ever realizing it. I never forgot that conversation.

You didn't have to follow her career to understand who she was. Her work ethic was its own folklore; everyone in the scene had a story about watching her rehearse in a hallway, rework a bit between sets, or stay long after a show to talk shop with whoever needed it.

What struck me most, though, was how she treated people. Not just comics with credits, but the servers running drinks, the door guy juggling IDs, and fans hoping for a photo. She gave each person the same level gaze, the same easy warmth—as if their presence mattered. There was nothing polished or self-congratulatory about it. She simply noticed people.

The green room at the Laughing Skull wasn't really a room at all. It was a narrow wedge of space painted a deep,

ambitious shade of red. Most nights, the usual tribe rotated through: comics pacing in circles, mouthing punchlines, dropping notes into their phones, or zoning out into that pre-show trance where you stare at a blank patch of carpet and pray a new closer materializes. Someone is always claiming the good seat—the one spot on the couch that didn't make you sink low enough to question your life choices.

On the weekends, the room changed. Even the air felt charged in a way that only happens when the comics you grew up watching suddenly exist in the same ten feet of space you're sitting in.

You'd walk in and find yourself shoulder-to-shoulder with Michael Ian Black, who, between sets, drifted into stories about his kids, about family life. It was disarming to hear the guy who built on sarcasm open up with such warmth. Or catch a glimpse of Maria Bamford adjusting her hair in the corner mirror; she had a way of leaning in when she spoke, her voice dropping to an almost secret-sharing hush.

Bobcat Goldthwait might be holding court, telling some story that made every person in earshot lean closer, or Theo Von throwing out an offhand comment that derailed everyone in the best way.

The intimacy of it never got old. One minute, you're a kid watching them from your couch at home. The next time you're trying not to spill a drink on their shoes. For a place barely bigger than a hallway, that green room held a decade of my life.

That one night, September 30, didn't feel remarkable at first. I sat tucked into my usual corner of the Laughing Skull's green room, headphones in, mentally scrolling through my set list that I'd refined twelve times that week. The club radiated its normal pre-show energy; I'd just restarted my hype track by Deftones, *My Own Summer (Shove It),* when I noticed someone walking toward me. No introduction, no crew trailing behind him, just a calm confidence that didn't need an entrance.

Chris Tucker.

He gave me a slight nod, and I nodded back, because what else do you do when Chris Tucker acknowledges your existence in a room barely larger than a walk-in pantry? He didn't launch into polite filler, we just...talked. Comfortable, unhurried, and almost like we'd known each other longer than the ten seconds it took him to cross into the room.

At one point, without thinking, I mentioned that my mom was a huge fan. His whole face lit up, warm and curious—like the conversation had opened another door.

"It's actually her birthday today," I added.

And that's when the night shifted from memorable to unforgettable.

He broke into a wide grin. "No way."

I nodded, because yes, way.

Before I could explain anything else, he held out his hand for my phone. No hesitation, no celebrity performance, just genuine curiosity. "What's her name?"

I told him.

Seconds later, he had the phone up to his ear, leaning back on that green room couch as if it was the most natural thing in the world.

"Hey, Mama Vicki! Happy birthday! Your son's out here doing his thing. Be proud!"

No buildup. No grand announcement. Just a legendary comic placing a call to my mother as casually as someone ordering takeout—delivering, in under ten seconds, the single most incredible birthday moment she'd ever had.

Afterward, I thanked him, though the words felt small compared to what he'd just given her. I doubt he realized the impact. That call didn't fade into the night or blend in with the dozens of stories she loved to retell. It etched itself into her memory like a favorite song.

Then they opened the curtains.

Showtime.

I stepped out and hit the audience with a quick five—just enough to get the wheels turning and the room warming up. Then came the moment I'd been sitting on for fifteen minutes. Grinning like I had a winning lottery ticket in my pocket, I dropped it: "We've got a special guest tonight. Please welcome the one and only...Mr. Chris Tucker!"

The place detonated. Cheers, gasps, people grabbing each other's arms like they'd seen a ghost. And then he walked out—cool as ever—and took over. By the time he wrapped, they were putty. Every line hit, every beat landed. I stood just offstage, watching a pro turn that tiny room into his personal playground.

And then came a blonde bombshell...

Sunglasses indoors, laughing at full volume like the concept of "indoor voice" had never applied to her.

Jennifer.

Jennifer Coolidge.

She looked like money—not the new, crisp kind, but the old, generational kind that owns property in every zipcode and doesn't apologize for it. Her lip gloss caught the light so perfectly, I'm convinced it had its own lighting crew. Her hair is voluminous. Ethereal. Possibly engineered by NASA. She moved through the green room with the kind of poise that made you wonder if she'd rehearsed it with a choreographer—but somehow, none of it felt forced.

She had a makeup artist trailing her, a guy with razor-sharp brows and the gentle hand of someone who's handled royal jewels. He dabbed at her face between takes like she was made of porcelain.

And even with the fame, the noise, the big-screen orbit around her, she stayed disarmingly chill. No pretense. Just this calm, confident cool that made the whole room loosen its shoulders. She had a way of talking to people that erased hierarchy—suddenly comics, staff, and the audience all felt part of a singular moment, the same laugh.

Marshall tapped me to emcee opening night to a packed room, the start of a weekend stacked with sold-out shows.

Saturday night, we found ourselves at The Clermont Lounge—Atlanta's most confusing landmark: part strip club, part dive bar, part senior showcase. The dancers were proudly in their late sixties and carried themselves with a confidence that only comes with age.

Jennifer walked through that place as if she'd been there before in another life. Nothing put-on. Nothing begged to be noticed. She just fit, and took the whole place with the

enthusiasm of someone arriving at precisely the kind of chaos they secretly hoped for.

She'd barely crossed the threshold, maybe thirty seconds in, when one of the dancers made her entrance. The woman, a very young sixty-two, was dressed head-to-toe as Little Bo Peep, bonnet and all, and she climbed straight onto the bar, which doubled as the stage. Then, without warming up the crowd or easing into it, she started smacking her own ass with her herding stick.

When it was her turn to order, she paused—just long enough to reel the whole room in. One hand on the bar, her glossed lips catching the amber light, gaze trailing down the line of bottles as if she were picking her co-star.

"Hmm..." she said, drawing it out like someone had missed their cue. Then finally, in that unmistakable honey-dipped voice:

"I'll have a vodka soda...with a lime, if you've got one."

She turned toward me, leaned in, eyes twinkling. "So...what's the weirdest thing you've seen in here, besides Little Bo Peep?"

I didn't even get the chance to answer.

Because just then, a woman named Blondie—Clermont royalty, unbothered icon—stepped into our orbit. She wore a platinum wig with enough shine to compete with every light in the building, paired with an outfit that delivered its own announcement...before she even opened her mouth.

She had on a puritan-white tank top that didn't so much "fit" as it *clung to the idea of fitting,* with glitter dusted across her chest. Blondie stood two feet away, clutching a half-finished PBR with the casual confidence of someone who'd already stolen the show. She grinned, brought the can to her chest, and flattened it between her boobs with mechanical precision.

Jennifer's eyes went wide. One hand to her heart.

"Oh...my God," Jennifer whispered, almost devotional. You'd think she'd just witnessed a religious event, proudly sponsored by Pabst Brewing Company.

THE CLOSET HAD A REVOLVING DOOR

I was standing on stages I used to imagine from my childhood bedroom, the ones I'd picture while staring at the ceiling and wondering how people ever got to live those kinds of lives. And yet, somewhere in the background of all that momentum was a call from my mom that screeched across my life like someone yanking the aux cord out mid-song.

Our call started harmless enough. She was in an unusually chatty mood where she'd cycle through names from my childhood, checking on people I hadn't thought about since graduation. I answered, filled in what I knew, and made up the rest—the usual.

Then her questions drifted into new territory.

"Is she married now?"

"What about her? Kids?"

She was circling something she couldn't quite grip, and then she went straight for it.

She asked me if I'd heard from *her*—using her full name with this bright certainty—the last girl I dated before coming out. "She was such a nice girl," my mom said, so sweet and sure of herself. "Is she seeing anyone now?"

The first time, I brushed it off.

The second time, I felt my shoulders tense.

It wasn't until the third or fourth time she brought up that girl that I started feeling irritated. Her repetition, her tone, felt pointed, almost intentional, like she was trying to steer me back toward a version of myself I'd already outgrown.

And then it clicked.

She wasn't hinting.

She wasn't judging.

She wasn't trying to "fix" anything.

She didn't remember.

That entire chapter, my coming out, the conversation we'd had, the complicated tenderness between us—got erased by her brain surgery. I sat there, phone to my ear, listening to her talk about a future that didn't exist. Wouldn't exist.

So then came the realization that I had to come out to my mom again.

A second premiere. The reboot nobody asked for.

Honestly, it felt like standing in front of a fire I'd already walked through once—only now, someone handed me a match and said, "Be a sport, and light it yourself."

The first time I came out, I did it on paper because saying

it out loud felt impossible. I stared at the words I'd written, trying to convince myself they belonged to me. They didn't. They sat on the page like they were auditioning for a role I wasn't ready to play.

But now, in my mid-twenties, everything had changed. I'd spent years working in entertainment and living in the city, surrounded by people who couldn't care less who anyone else was attracted to. It wasn't even noteworthy; being gay was as casual as ordering a latte. More importantly, I felt steady in who I was.

And yes, I did have peace in my heart. But peace doesn't always cushion the truth when family is part of the equation.

I already had a trip to visit her scheduled. Leesburg wasn't far, just over three hours south of Atlanta—but it felt like another planet. Every mile I drove toward South Georgia, the man I'd worked so hard to become blurred in the rearview, and all that remained was the scared kid who knew he was different—and just couldn't say why.

My family didn't hate who I was—they just didn't recognize the terrain. They'd never spent real time around anyone gay. Not at work. Not at church. Not in the circles they trusted. For them, I was the first page of a book they didn't know existed, and the first time the story came without fear or judgment.

I never doubted their love, but there were borders around it, soft at the surface, firm once you bumped against them. Their support came through in everyday ways: calls, check-ins, the kinds of concerns families share without thinking. But the moment my personal life entered the conversation, something closed off. No one said anything harsh. No one said anything at all.

When my sister introduced the man who would become her husband, he stepped into our world with no hesitation required. One Christmas, everyone treated him as if he'd been there for years. That kind of easy acceptance wasn't waiting for me. I knew it.

I turned off I-75 south exit at 99, the road blurred into one long stretch, and I couldn't tell if I was moving too fast or not moving at all. A million different thoughts tore through my head in a pile-up, none of them waiting their turn, and all of them convinced they were urgent.

I was feeling all of the pain from the first time I told my mom the truth. The memory of that—seeing her for the first time, knowing I'd just broken something I couldn't repair, hit me hard. My hands tightened around the wheel until my knuckles blanched, and a hard pressure climbed through my ribs with each inhale.

I needed to stop before I lost control entirely.

So I veered into the first gas station I saw and pulled into a space with more force than intention. Once the gear clicked into park, my head dropped forward, and a noise slipped out that I sincerely hope no one in the parking lot heard.

My mom had already endured more than most people face, but the brain surgery rewrote her in ways none of us could anticipate. Changes that went far beyond the physical recovery; something at her core rearranged itself.

And now, this.

I sat there, staring through the windshield, trying to

convince myself to move. When I finally turned the key and eased back onto the road, it felt less like composure and more like stubborn momentum. The last thirty minutes toward my mom's house stretched in front of me, the highway cutting through land that never seemed to change. Sameness pressed in from both sides, always making the drive feel like a loop that refused to end.

I eased into her neighborhood and followed the familiar curve of the street until her house came into view. I rested my hands on the steering wheel and closed my eyes, and a quiet prayer slipped out. Then I drew a deep breath, stepped out, and crossed the small walkway toward the front door.

After I dropped my bag in the guest room, I found her in the kitchen and floated the idea of dinner. She agreed, and we ended up at the Mellow Mushroom—neutral territory.

The server had barely reached the table before I asked for a vodka soda. Mom scanned the menu with her usual patience and went with a sweet tea. Across from us, the wall stretched from one end of the restaurant to the other, and an entire timeline of music painted in wild color—I loved it.

Elvis anchored on the far side, hips cocked, frozen in a pose that never lost confidence. Further down, the neon geometry from the Blood Sugar Sex Magik era cut through the collage, the Red Hot Chili Peppers captured in that moment when their sound blew up in the nineties. A few panels later, Gwen Stefani stared out in Rock Steady boldness, marking No Doubt's shift into the early-2000s.

Albany didn't offer much, and this mural was proof of that. It was the only thing in the town with a pulse. It didn't belong in a place that still clung to the comfort of its old power structures. Albany liked its routines untouched, its circles closed, and its worldview frozen somewhere decades behind the rest of the country. That mural always captivated me, but it also made everything around it feel dated.

I eased into the conversation with small talk, sticking to the lanes that never stirred anything up—my drive, comedy, the dog hair in my truck. While mom answered, my focus kept drifting to the mural, Janis Joplin with her glasses lifted towards the ceiling, Hendrix caught mid-solo. I kept staring at them, wishing they could lend me a little backbone.

When it felt right, I nudged her toward her favorite subject and mentioned the last girl I'd gone out with. Mom's whole expression warmed. Right then, the server dropped off our drinks—perfect timing. She lifted her sweet tea and told me she couldn't wait to see grandbabies from me someday.

I gulped my vodka soda big enough to qualify as a cry for help, then I cut her off quickly. Too quickly.

Because I knew if I let her keep talking, something in me would give, so I leaned in a little and said, "Mom...about five years ago, I wrote you a letter." The words came out tighter than I intended. "You got pretty emotional when you read it. Do you remember that?"

She paused, then drifted into a gentle shake of her head. She started naming moments she couldn't place anymore— running through old stories she once rattled off without thinking. After the third one, I reached across the table and rested my hand over hers.

"It's okay," I said, "You're here. You're alive. That's what matters."

In my periphery, The Beatles lined up in perfect formation; R.E.M. was watching me from their corner... every set of painted eyes felt fixed on me. These legends were my audience, waiting for the truth.

My body wouldn't move, held in the same stillness that froze every face on that wall. I drew in a deep breath and pushed ahead anyway.

"Mom, I need to tell you something," I said. "I need you to understand...we've already had this conversation once."

She didn't answer. Her hands stilled, her eyes fixed on me, giving me her full attention as if we were the only people in the room.

"I'm gay."

My eyes bounced between hers and the mural on the wall behind her, as if it mattered.

I took a long sip of my drink to fill the silence, then held my mom's gaze and gave a slight nod—an unspoken invitation for her to say something. Anything.

Mom reached for her lemon wedge on the rim of her glass, squeezed it into her tea, then met my eyes. I could see her replaying my words, sorting through them, checking whether she'd overlooked an important piece of context.

She finally spoke. "Are you sure?"

I didn't have a chance to answer. The server arrived with our plates, sliding them onto the table with practiced cheer.

I focused on the steam rising off my food in soft spirals, grateful for the interruption. I wasn't mad at her—but I hated that we were here again, starting from the same place all over again. And I knew, even if she didn't say it, her heart was splitting open all over again—she was simply physically incapable of showing it.

I stared down at my plate, a slice of cheese pizza, edges curling, dusted with a layer of parmesan cheese, and the crushed red pepper I kept shaking on just to delay speaking.

"Mom, I'm twenty-five—almost twenty-six. I've spent my whole life trying to be anything other than who I actually am, and now, I feel like I've finally started to catch up. Because I didn't even know who that person was."

I worked on the paper wrapper from my straw until it gave way, breaking into soft scraps that stuck to my fingertips. I kept going anyway, piece after piece, anything to keep my hands busy.

Then, I looked up. "No one made me gay. This isn't something you caused."

I tried to tell her I was seeing someone, but I could feel it—the line had been pulled far enough for one conversation. She was uncomfortable. Not angry, just sorting through more than she could say. Emotion didn't register on her face the way it used to, and for once, that worked in my favor. I didn't need a significant response; I simply needed calm.

"Trey, I love you no matter what," she said finally. "I just worry about you. I don't want someone to hurt you because of this."

She meant it. In her mind, I was marked, as if being honest about who I was made me an open target.

I only managed a few bites of pizza.

Our conversation left me feeling stranded in a way I didn't expect. I didn't realize it, but I'd held on to this small,

impossible daydream where my mom leaned in and asked about my boyfriend, when she'd get to meet him, how we met, and whether he made me happy. Some part of me wanted it so badly I nearly believed it could unfold right there at the table.

I knew it could've gone far worse. No threat of being pushed out of her life, no lecture waiting to corner me. But I also knew nothing would open that door. It stayed sealed, the same as before.

Coming out the first time drained me.

Doing it again was hell.

EROSION

When I came out to my mom the second time, I was actually dating someone. At twenty-five, I swan-dived into what I was sure was a great love story. He carried that wounded-genius energy that people like himself write tortured ballads about.

He spoke in metaphors. Smiled like he'd already survived his own personal firestorm, written cathartic essays about the experience, and then used the leftover heat to warm the room. Every story he shared about his past arrived as a carefully curated tragedy—betrayals amassed on heartbreak, all threaded with reminders that everyone he'd ever trusted had failed him.

Most people spotted the red flags. I fluffed them, turned them into throw pillows, and settled right in.

I wanted to be the exception—the one who didn't leave.

So I stayed.

That was my first mistake.

Four months in, I signed the lease on a stunning loft.

He was "getting back on his feet," and I was still drunk on the fantasy.

Mistake number two.

We moved in on a Monday morning.

There was no buildup. One minute, I was unpacking dishes, and the next, the apartment was full of paramedics running past me, the dispatcher's voice still bleeding through my phone. Because by that afternoon, he'd taken an entire bottle of Xanax and dropped to the floor, because apparently the emotional strain of moving into an apartment someone else paid for was just too much.

When he finally opened his eyes about twenty-four hours later, in the hospital, he locked onto me and said he'd done it because I wasn't giving him enough of my time.

Naturally, it was my fault.

That scene was only the preview. For the next year and a half, he drafted a storyline where he suffered beautifully, and I ruined everything. He rewrote each chapter until I became the villain he needed.

No matter what I handed over—money, pep talks I wasn't trained to give, the square footage of my own peace, the parts of myself that used to speak up—all disappeared into his emotional black hole. I became fluent in saying nothing in precisely the wrong way.

He'd tell me I was selfish. I worked too much. Being with me made him want to die.

No volume.

The delivery came while he bent over to tie his shoes, fingers looping the laces. His attention stayed on the floor, his tone flat, conversational-level calm, as if he were commenting on the forecast rather than detonating our evening. Not even a glance in my direction.

Then came the rest, he insisted people tolerated me solely because I hovered near comics who actually mattered. Without them, I was just another body in the room.

The worst part was how quietly his voice became my own. I caught myself repeating his lines—little mantras I never agreed to, only now they came out in my tone, which made them harder to ignore.

Day after day, the script wore me down until I finally heard something that didn't sound like him at all. A sentence that rose from somewhere he couldn't touch.

And it wasn't a punchline.

"Get the fuck out of my loft."

After I kicked him out, he ended up in Kara's place, someone I'd introduced him to, another comic, conveniently in the same complex—truly a bold relocation.

So yeah, he was gone, technically.

Three weeks had passed without a single message from him, and my apartment felt livable again—mine in a way it hadn't since the day he arrived with his boxes and his drama. I'd poured years of work into affording that place, and this was the first time I could move through it without tension trailing behind me.

I started going out again, letting myself talk to people

without stressing who it might upset. I wasn't walking into a room wondering if my friendliness made me the problem. I've never chased attention; I just reach for connection. But he had reduced that into something selfish and performative.

Being around friends reminded me that nothing was wrong with me for showing up in the world with energy. Just me, moving through the world without needing a permission slip for my own personality. I hadn't recognized how absent that feeling had been until it came back.

And I was genuinely excited for the weekend ahead. The Laughing Skull had Marc Maron headlining; he's sharp, introspective, and one of the OG long-form interview podcasts: *WTF with Marc Maron.*

Coincidentally, my sister arrived the day before the shows. She'd come to Atlanta from Leesburg for a work conference, and timing finally lined up for us to see each other without a holiday or crisis pulling the strings. I was looking forward to it—real time together, catching up without rushing.

But the minute I sat down at the restaurant, my phone lit up. His name filled the screen over and over: *When are you coming back? I need to get the rest of my stuff.*

A second later, the phone rang. I flipped it face down and muted it before my sister could notice the distraction in me.

The "urgent" item he needed was a computer cord, the same type of cord you can replace in ten minutes at Best Buy if you actually get off your ass. Yet, he'd fired off sixteen messages about it—out of the blue.

I had no idea which horse of the apocalypse would be waiting for me later, so I left my phone on silent and untouched until I pulled into the gate, parked, and finally gave in to checking it.

My messages were flooded.

He'd started with: "Always has to be on your terms, Trey."

Two minutes later: "Where the fuck is my cord?"

Followed by an apology that read like a hostage note, "I'm sorry, I didn't mean it like that...I just had a bad day, and I miss you."

Then, "btw, I know what you're doing. I've seen everything."

It played out like three strangers commandeered his phone and spent the evening arguing with each other through my number. And then the thread closed on a message that eclipsed the rest:

"I see you pulling in."

Sent four minutes earlier. Which meant he wasn't guessing—he'd actually been watching.

I'd been home *maybe* fifteen minutes. My phone lit up with a stack of missed calls that could've passed for a medical emergency. By the seventh one, I answered just to shut it down. I forced my voice into that steady, calm tone he responded to, but still very direct.

"What..." I asked. "What do you need from me?"

He just said my name. "Trey."

Flat. Cold. That Hannibal Lecter calm—right before the teeth come out.

"I saw you pull in," he said. "You've been back a while and still didn't answer or respond to my texts."

Then he snapped.

"WHY ARE YOU LYING? YOU'RE A FUCKING LIAR!"

I couldn't even figure out the offence, unless failing to drop everything for a computer cord now counted as deception. But he'd already taken off. His rage didn't wait for clarity; it surged through the phone—random accusations firing in every direction with escalating force. It was the sound of a man trying to rewrite a story only he could see.

I pressed my fingers to my temple, and that's when I heard it: his voice twice.

Once in my ear.

And once...on the other side of my door.

I thought I was safe.

The door was locked.

I had the key. I had the backup key.

When I kicked him out, I made damn sure of it.

What I didn't know—what I couldn't have imagined— was that he'd already made himself a copy.

The whole door frame shook under his fists, a staccato warning that he wasn't backing down.

Then I heard it—the mechanical turn that didn't belong to me—*click*. The lock gave way, and the door blasted open.

He crossed the threshold with a blank expression, eyes wide but empty, his body propelling itself across the room in a frantic rush. It felt less like he'd entered and more like something had slipped inside wearing his face.

I said something—I still can't remember. Whatever it was, it lit the fuse.

He seized me at the shoulders and hurled me from the

hallway into the bedroom wall. The hit knocked the breath from my lungs. Before I could find my footing, he dragged me sideways, my back scraping across the corner of the wall, tearing along bone like it wanted to take skin with it.

I tried to stand.

He ripped the floor lamp from its base, gripping it by the neck, and drove it into my torso with enough force to send me crashing through the drywall that had already caved under the earlier hit.

I lunged for the narrow opening between the pillar and the wall.

Didn't make it.

He caught me from behind, slammed me into the hallway wall, and clamped both hands around my throat.

He squeezed hard.

The world tightened to a pin-sized point. No hallway, no color, no depth until all I could see was his grip and the small patch of wall behind him.

Only one thought hammered through my head: If I go under now, that's it.

I beat my fists against the wall, a desperate attempt to make noise, any noise. I forced a scream past his hands, the sound tearing up my throat just to get out.

"Shut the fuck up," he snarled, yanking one hand off my throat just long enough to slap it over my mouth, smothering whatever sound I had left.

By the grace of God, Felicia, my next-door neighbor, was home. She heard every muffled yell bleed through the wall. She came straight to my door, knocked once, then pushed it open.

Her voice at the doorway snapped him out of whatever state he was in. He dropped his hands, stepped back fast, and bolted down the hall. Police arrive about fifteen minutes later. I told them exactly what happened. They cuffed him outside and took him off the property.

The next morning, I showed up for my haircut. Ashley, my hair stylist, took one look at the marks circling my neck and didn't ask a single question—just told me to run to Walgreens, grab concealer that matched my skin, and come right back. When I returned, she guided my hand through blending it in, treating it the way someone might hide a hickey, not the aftermath of an assault.

I went onstage that night and performed as if nothing had happened. The weekend was solid, I even recorded a podcast with Marc, and acted like my neck wasn't still tender under a layer of drugstore concealer.

And that leads to my third mistake: not pressing charges. At twenty-six, I honestly believed calling the police on my ex, watching them take him away in cuffs, would be enough to scare him straight, that the shock of it would be some turning point.

I confused confrontation with consequence.

They aren't the same. They never were.

The regret really hit me when Kara, his roommate and my friend, told me what he'd been doing behind the scenes. He'd installed spyware on my Mac. Every keystroke recorded. Screenshots. My webcam feeds him a live window into my life. He never denied it; he *showed* her. Sat there bragging, pulling up images and clips of me like he was scrolling through his personal highlight reel.

And while he was still monitoring me months later, he was also using Kara's name as his personal bank account. Credit cards. Loans. He even manipulated her into signing for a Smart Car. She never saw a cent from him—not one.

There wasn't even space to catch up to what had happened before the next crisis hit. My mom's headaches returned.

Her doctor ordered another MRI.

When the results came back, the words hit like a punch: two new aneurysms.

Everything after that blurred. All I could think was, *here we go again.*

They set her procedure for late July at Emory University Hospital in Atlanta. This time, she had a better shot. New technology had changed the landscape. And because of where the aneurysms sat, the neurosurgeon didn't have to open her skull again. Instead, he would thread a thin catheter through a blood vessel in her femoral artery and guide it all the way to her brain.

Once it reached the aneurysm, he'd release tiny platinum coils to pack it from the inside, cutting off the blood flow before it had a chance to rupture.

After the surgery, her recovery settled into a rhythm of follow-ups and post-op appointments. My sister and I decided Mom should stay with me in my loft in Atlanta's Old Fourth Ward neighborhood until she could drive again.

So, it was me and Mom. Just like it used to be

During that same period, I lost my job. Another blow, one I didn't have the bandwidth to absorb.

LEESBURG: A MASTER CLASS IN LOW EXPECTATIONS

By 2012, everything was gone: the career I'd worked for, the savings I leaned on, the sense of direction I pretended I had. My only plan was simple: stay upright.

All year, I scrambled to keep my apartment. I picked up whatever hustle I could and crossed lines I still can't bring myself to put on paper. Every month felt like a countdown. I woke up low, stayed low, and slid even deeper as the months piled on. My path didn't disappear; it blew apart, and after years of trying to make the right choices, I hit a point where I stopped caring.

The drinking that used to be social turned into maintenance. The party drugs stopped being "weekend." By late summer, the sober parts of my day felt accidental.

When I couldn't renew my lease, it was the final shove. I packed what I could into my car and left Atlanta behind. On September 30, my mom's birthday, I rolled into Leesburg with everything I could fit in my truck, intending to reset my life.

Leesburg felt like the ghost of a sitcom that never got picked up—outdated sets and a laugh track triggered by anything outside the norm. I felt disoriented, as if I'd somehow fallen through a crack in time and landed in someone else's America—one where I had to tuck parts of myself away to avoid drawing the wrong kind of attention.

In South Georgia, I stuck out so hard it was almost a public service announcement. Everyone else looked like they'd just come from church or Tractor Supply, and there I was— tattoos, "city clothes, giant sunglasses, and a hairstyle that said, "I don't fix fences—I drink espresso and overshare onstage."

I made it over twenty days before I bailed and headed back to Atlanta.

Not to move, just long enough to have a night that kept a piece of me alive.

It was late October at the Tabernacle, my favorite venue in the city. The best part was getting to go with someone who'd known me since the days when we were both broke twenty-year-olds working retail, trying to display ties around each other's necks and laughing through shifts we barely survived. Jess Forkel and I bonded instantly, same kind of humor, same struggle coming out to our moms, same sense that we didn't quite yet fit the mold we were handed.

By then, she'd built herself a whole radio career, producing a hit morning show. And Forkel gave me one of the most

incredible gifts I've ever gotten: a chance to meet Alanis Morissette backstage.

Meeting Alanis felt surreal. She wasn't rushing anyone, just moving person to person with an ease that made the whole room soften. She hugged people, posed for photos, listened—really listened—and carried an energy that made you feel like you weren't wasting her time. Thirteen-year-old me would've shut down completely—full system failure, blue screen, someone unplug me and plug me back in. Thank God I was older.

To keep myself from rambling, I handed her a note instead. I couldn't tell you word for word what I wrote, but it was about growing up gay, about feeling swallowed up by loneliness at times, and how her music had been a steady presence through it.

And that night, surrounded by all that noise and bliss and possibility—my friend reignited something in me I'd let go dim. A part of myself I'd shut down, flickered back to life.

Two days later, when I got home, I walked into something I wasn't prepared for.

My mom sat in her chair with two black eyes so severe that it looked like she'd taken a beating. The bruises weren't faint or passing—they swallowed the space around her eyes.

Her balance had been unreliable since the surgeries, but seeing her like that...slashed through every bit of denial I'd been holding onto.

I'd only been in South Georgia for a few weeks, but it was enough to confirm that the mom I grew up with, the one who noticed everything, who ran circles around any problem, who anticipated needs before anyone spoke, was definitely gone.

APRIL LEFT IN SILENCE

Two days after my twenty-eighth birthday, six months into my exile, South Georgia had worked its way into every part of me—my clothes, my lungs, probably even my personality. I pulled into my mom's driveway, tapped the brake, and cut the engine, already dreading what I knew was waiting.

The second I cracked open the car door, they charged: gnats, thousands of them, confident and organized, coming at me as if I'd barged into a family gathering uninvited. They went straight for my face—eyes, ears, even my mouth. I swatted at the air like I was getting jumped in the driveway.

Didn't matter. The gnats didn't retreat. They simply formed up again and came back swinging.

I glanced at the porch. My mom's hanging basket was doing the most—blooms spilling over the rim, competing

for attention, tossing out color and attitude, feeling the heat. Everything she planted thrived without trying.

Meanwhile, sweat crept down my spine, my shirt sticking to me in places that I didn't approve of. I crossed the driveway, fished out my keys, and slid one into the front-door lock.

"Atticus! Ollie!"

Right on cue: one shrill bark from Ollie, then Atticus' even higher-pitched follow-up, always a beat behind, like he thought noise trumped timing.

"Hey, Trey, how's everything? Did you have a good day?" Her voice floated in from the kitchen—easy, warm—her soft Southern drawl could make a scolding sound like a lullaby.

She stood at the stove, moving the spoon in slow circles like she had all the time in the world. When she lifted her head, her eyes caught mine, already smiling. "Come give me a hug."

"Just fixing some dinner—soup tonight," she said, giving it the same enthusiasm most people reserved for restaurant reservations. "We missed you!" The way she said it told me she meant every word, never mind that I'd only been gone a few hours on a mid-shift.

"Good, Mom," I answered, the response coming out of habit more than I thought. I stepped in for a quick hug, her version of grounding me, a reset that never needed explanation.

I eased back toward the hallway. "I'll be right back. Just need a minute to shake the day off." What I really needed was the small break a cigarette offered. My own little intermission, the space between the world outside and the world she created inside that kitchen.

"You're not going out for a smoke, are you Trey?" she called after me, her voice carrying that familiar blend—soft around the edges, but laced with the sort of concern that made me feel twelve again.

I turned just enough to catch the expression I knew by muscle memory, and it hovered somewhere between *I raised you better and please don't die prematurely.*

"Mom," I exhaled, trying to let the whole conversation out with it. "It's not new. And yes—I am. You know that."

The impatience slipped out before I could stop it, so I tossed in a smirk. "Besides...you smoke."

Not my most vigorous defense, but a solid deflection and a familiar beat in a conversation we'd repeated a hundred times.

She sighed, shaking her head gently. "I know, honey. I wish you wouldn't. I just love you, that's all."

"Back in a sec," I called over my shoulder, already moving before the words finished leaving my mouth.

In my room, I reached for one of my smoking hoodies— the sacrificial ones. The fabric carried a faint, stale trace of every other night just like this, which was the whole point. I kept the rest of my clothes safe from the smell I pretended didn't bother me.

Hoodie in hand, I retraced my steps through the living room. She was right where I knew she'd be: settled into her sunny-yellow chair, the TV casting a soft glow across her cheeks. Her bowl of soup rested on the tray, steam lifting in gentle wisps as she stirred, her focus making the moment feel slower.

At her feet, Atticus and Ollie sat poised like tiny soldiers

on duty, their attention fixed on the spoon as if one stray drip might determine the fate of the evening. Their heads tilted in perfect sync each time her wrist moved, both of them convinced patience was their best strategy.

I moved toward the sliding glass door and eased it open. The room's cool fell away as I stepped out onto the screened-in porch, letting the door settle back into place with a muted click that always felt like crossing a boundary—her world on one side, mine on the other.

Flyleaf's new song, "New Horizons," blasted from my iPhone, filling the porch with a burst of sound that felt bigger than the space itself. The box fan in the corner puttered along, doing what it could in the spring heat, but still it felt like its blades were turning without urgency.

I leaned against the railing and watched the sky work through its evening colors—violet easing into pink, then dimming toward deeper blues as the day lost its grip. For a few minutes, I let the view pull me in. Leesburg didn't offer much, but the sunsets here always tried their best.

When the cigarette burned down to the filter, I flicked the last bit into the tray and pushed off the railing. Stepping back inside, the cooler air met me halfway. "How's the soup?" I called, already veering toward the sink.

The smell of smoke assaulted my hand, settling into the creases of my fingers. I turned on the tap and scrubbed hard, watching the water run over my knuckles and swirl down the drain. I hated how the scent refused to budge. I kept washing anyway, muscle memory thinking for me.

I glanced toward the living room. From the kitchen, her

chair was out of sight, but *Entertainment Tonight* played on, spilling celebrity news to no one.

She was probably in the bathroom. She always kept a mug of water nearby and constantly refilled it.

I stepped out of the kitchen and turned the corner.

And in an instant, the room didn't meet me the way it should. Everything was wrong.

It took a moment for my mind to line up the scene in front of me. The tray lay on its side, the bowl nowhere in sight. Soup streaked across the rug in uneven tracks, sinking into the fibers, gathering around shattered pieces of ceramic scattered at her feet.

She was on the hardwood where the rug ended, caught in a motion that never finished. Her nightgown was twisted, one arm stretched forward, fingers hovering over space. Her mouth was parted—just enough to show a word had been forming and never made it out.

A sound tore out of me before I realized it belonged to me when it was already ricocheting off the walls. "Mom! Mom!"

The dogs rushed the spilled soup, tails cutting quick arcs behind them, tongues darting as they tried to claim every drop. They circled in erratic bursts, panting, pacing, paws tapping across the floor—wholly unaware of the disaster unfolding inches away.

But she stayed exactly where she'd fallen.

Not a single movement. Not even a breath, I could convince myself I saw.

I shoved them aside, harder than I meant to. "Move!" The shout sent them skittering back, startled and confused.

I dropped beside her so fast the room spun. My palms hit the floor, then her.

My fingers were jelly. They kept slipping as I tried to find the right spot on her neck. I pressed anyway, searching for a thump I could hang onto. Nothing. I moved to her wrist, the same wrist that used to brush my hair off my forehead when I was sick.

Still nothing.

"Mom—Mom, come on—wake up!" The words spilled out of me. I grabbed her shoulder and shook with everything I had. Her arms slid across the floor, limp and unresponsive, the way a doll's arm moves when a child drops it.

The TV kept rambling in the corner, oblivious—some news story I'd heard a hundred times. It didn't pause, didn't soften, didn't register that anything in the house had changed. The rug sat perfectly still beneath us, every thread lying in place, as if the room refused to acknowledge what was happening.

For half a second, the normalcy of it all messed with me. Everything looked the same as when I walked in. It made me question whether I'd misunderstood what I saw, whether my mind was playing tricks to fill a moment I couldn't process.

I pushed off the floor and staggered toward the kitchen, moving too fast for my legs to catch up. My foot slid, and I caught the counter with both hands, gripping it so hard my knuckles cracked.

The phone. I needed my phone.

Where the fuck was it?

My vision jerked from one surface to the next; everything

was too bright and too blurry at once. Counters, cabinets, the fridge handle—none of it registered as helpful. I dragged my hand across the countertop, knocking into a glass, a set of keys, anything in the way, praying my fingers would reach the one thing that mattered.

When I found it, I grabbed it so fast it nearly slipped right back out of my grip. The screen swam the moment I tried to focus on it, letters stretching, numbers doubling. My thumb dragged across the glass, but nothing connected to where I aimed. My brain fired instructions in perfect order, but the rest of me was a second behind.

At last, my thumb hit the call button. The ring shot out of the speaker in a pitch that cut straight through the room and up the side of my head. My whole body locked onto that tone, with every single nerve on the same frantic frequency.

"Please," I whispered into the phone, barely hearing myself. "Please...please...", over and over. "Pick up. Pick up."

I dropped beside her again, the phone pressed to my ear. My hand went back to her wrist on instinct, even though I already knew what I'd felt the first time. I pushed harder anyway, moving my fingers along the same path I'd checked seconds earlier, hoping I'd somehow missed something.

"911, what's your emergency?"

"I need an ambulance—my mom isn't breathing." Words came out in pieces, never fully forming. I tried again, stammering, "I-I stepped out for five minutes...and now she's on the floor...and she won't respond. Please help me!"

"The address..." My mouth went dry. "One-four...it's...

The rest of the numbers scattered the second I tried to

grab them. I wanted to pull them back into order, but they kept slipping, slipping, slipping. My own street—my own house—and I couldn't get it out.

"How much longer?" I asked, my voice shaking so hard it barely sounded like mine. I didn't wait for whatever she was about to say—I couldn't. Everything in me was already sprinting ahead of her.

"Please," I said, the word stumbling out, "Please, I'll do anything. Just save her. Please. Hurry!"

The begging poured out of me before I knew where to aim it: the operator, God, the walls, my mom. I didn't care who heard it. I just needed someone to do something.

Her voice came through the receiver, maddeningly calm. "Place your hands on her chest—one on top of the other."

I lowered my hands. The first press stole whatever breath I had left. My arms shook from the effort, or maybe it was the shock, or adrenaline, but I kept pushing—counting in my head, losing track, starting again. The only thing that existed in that moment was the rise and fall of my own force against her stillness.

"Keep going," the operator urged.

I did. My palms burned. I leaned my body into it, trying to give her everything I had. Nothing in her moved back. Nothing responded.

"You're doing great. I need you to stay calm and tell me when you complete thirty compressions," the operator said.

I wasn't sure what number I was on. I just kept pressing until my arms gave out and I had to reset, bracing my hands again, restarting the count, praying for the slightest sign that she was coming back to me.

"Come on, Mom," I whispered through my teeth. "Please."

The floor dug into my knees, and sweat dripped into my eyes. The operator's voice kept guiding me through the next set, but my mind was stuck in the same desperate loop: Move your hands. Push again. Don't let her go.

I ran to the front door and yanked it open. "Help me!" I screamed into the darkness. "Please, someone help us!"

Immediately, I spun back around and dropped beside her again, planting my hands where the operator told me and pushing until my arms shook. Everything outside that tiny circle—her body, my hands, the phone on speaker—faded out.

Tears smeared my vision, and as I leaned into the subsequent compression, something moved at the edge of my sight—a woman appeared in the doorway, outlined by the porch light behind her. I didn't recognize her, but she walked inside without hesitation, crossing the room like she'd been in that house a hundred times.

"I'm Mo," she said, her eyes sweeping over everything before settling on my mom. "Tell me what's happening. I live across the street. We just moved in."

There wasn't a trace of panic in her expression—only purpose. She moved toward us in one quick motion, already lowering herself to the floor, already bracing to help, already in it with me.

My mouth couldn't even keep up with what my mind was

trying to force out. I kept talking, chasing the story, trying to make her understand, trying to make it make sense.

Mo didn't flinch. She didn't tell me to breathe or start over. She stayed engaged, listening to me in a way that made the room feel a little less out of control.

"You're okay," she said. "You're not alone."

She didn't need to say anything more. I believed her.

For a second, her voice was the only thing connecting me to my body. Then new voices rushed from the outside, louder and faster than before. The calm Mo brought into the house collided with the hurried movement behind her—boots crossing the threshold, equipment rattling, strangers calling instructions to each other as they filled the living room around us.

I felt Mo's hand press gently to my arm, guiding me back so they could reach my mom. Every movement had a purpose, but everything hit me in uneven flashes: a uniform bending beside her, another setting something down on the floor, red lights painting the couch, the walls, the faces caught mid-laugh in the photos on the mantle—in and out of something that didn't feel like home.

Voices rose, instructions followed, but it all slid past me in pieces. They worked around me anyway.

My focus was on one place.

The woman who used to retell my birth story every single year—and had done it again less than forty-eight hours earlier, standing beside me in the kitchen while we laughed about how old I was getting, with that bright smile, now lay in front of me.

"6:42 AM," she'd say, tapping the numbers into the air with her finger. Her eyes would warm at the corners, always in the same spot in the story. "You came out stubborn and perfect." And then she'd pause, holding that moment between us, savoring it in the way only a mother can.

She called me her miracle baby.

Now her eyes were open and still, but the spark was gone. No crinkles at the corners. No voice calling my name. Just the shape of her face without her inside it.

They lifted my mom on a stretcher, and then she was gone.

The ambulance pulled away, its siren thinning out as it turned down the street. Red lights flickered across the houses on our street, washing over windows, porches, the same lawns people would step onto in the morning without knowing the world had come apart inside mine.

BE QUIET AND DRIVE

But I couldn't drive. I couldn't even think.

My sister was hours away—two and a half hours away on spring break with her husband and kids. Leesburg wasn't home to me. It wasn't even familiar. I'd been there six months and still needed a GPS just to get to the grocery store.

So I called Nicole.

A colleague-turned-friend from Pier One—the Assistant Store Manager who always carried warmth in her smile that could make anything feel less crushing. Not family. Not someone obligated to pick up. But she answered on the first ring.

I tried to speak, but everything tangled together—breath, panic, grief. Whatever came out barely qualified as words.

She didn't need me to make sense of it.

Her voice drifted through the phone with that warm, Southern sway she carried everywhere; soft on the vowels, light on the consonants, each syllable easing out with a gentleness that almost felt musical. The kind of voice that could settle a frantic customer or soothe a crying child without her even trying.

"I'm on my way." That's all I heard.

When I hung up, I knew Nicole would be at my mom's house within ten minutes, maybe less.

Everything collided at once—fear, guilt, disbelief—so fast my mind couldn't keep up. It felt impossible to hold even one of them, and somehow they were all there, demanding something from me I didn't have.

I needed it to stop.

I opened the fridge and saw the bottle of white wine from the night before—three-quarters full. I pulled the cork out and tipped it back, just straight from the bottle, trying to drown out the panic climbing through my body, trying to quiet the part of me screaming that I'd failed her.

I didn't need to be in the ambulance to know.

I'd lived this drill too many times. But it wasn't another round of the same nightmare. My body knew it before my mind would admit it.

The wine wasn't touching it.

I set the bottle down and checked my phone.

Still time.

I ran to my room, ground up a bud, packed a bowl with weed with hands that wouldn't stay steady, and pulled.

Hard. Until my lungs burned.

There's no way this was real.

Exhale.

It's a mistake. This *has to be* a mistake.

Another pull, harder.

They'll call before I even reach the hospital—that's what I kept telling myself. They'll say we got it wrong. Some part of me clung to that—this impossible hope that someone would undo the moment I'd just lived.

Waiting by the window felt endless, the yard swallowed in darkness until a pair of headlights finally swept across it. Nicole's hunter-green Honda CR-V eased into the driveway, familiar in a way that made the night feel even more unreal.

The door clicked shut behind me as I stepped outside. Warm night air met me, thick with the smell of grass and the humidity that never really leaves in South Georgia. That wine bottle dangled from my left hand, obvious and out of place. Nicole climbed out of her car, and by her expression, something told me she already understood more than I'd managed to say.

I folded into her like the whole night funneled me into that moment, into her arms, where everything finally gave out. She held on and guided me to the passenger seat without asking me for anything.

The drive to the hospital comes back in pieces—quick flashes. Headlights sweeping across the highway, then vanishing into stretches of dark. Nicole's hands are on the wheel. The soft drawl of her voice was trying to comfort me.

I'd never fallen apart like that. My face stayed wet, eyes burning, tears running faster than my hands could catch them, spilling into my beard and soaking Nicole's passenger seat with every cry that broke loose. The wine bottle stayed wedged between my knees—barely a swallow left in it.

Out of the dark, the hospital doors came into view—too bright, too polished, their glow stretching across the asphalt as if the entire building were bracing for me. Nicole pulled up to the ER entrance and let me out so she could park, her headlights sweeping past me as she drove off.

My phone vibrated in my pocket. Digging for it felt impossible; my hands wouldn't cooperate, adrenaline and alcohol fighting each other in my bloodstream.

By the time I pressed it to my ear, my sister's voice broke through that bright, hospital polish.

"We're on our way."

In the background, I could hear road noise—doors shutting, voices, movement, life still in motion on their end, while mine sat frozen outside the ER.

"Two hours," she said.

I pressed the phone tighter to my ear, trying to pull her closer through the connection, trying to make the distance shrink even a little.

"I love you—just get here. Please get here. Be careful."

My leg wouldn't stay still. It kept jerking, tapping, pushing against the sidewalk faster than I could rein it in. There was too much inside me—too much charge, too much panic—with no place to put any of it, so it leaked out through whatever part of my body would move.

She'll bounce back.

She always does.

I ran those words through my mind on a loop, chasing them, and trying to force them into something tangible.

The ER doors split open. A rush of sterile air pushed out toward me, cold, chemical, and too clean for what I'd just come from. It hit my face hard enough to pull me out of my head and remind me that I was standing in a place where lives turned on a dime.

Then he appeared.

A doctor stepped through the opening, and the white of his coat caught the overhead lights in a way that stopped everything inside me. He didn't say a word. He didn't have to. The expression on his face carried more truth than anything he could've spoken aloud.

One look, and the floor under me changed forever.

"We got a heartbeat," he said, his voice stoic in a way that didn't match the shape of his eyes. "For a moment...in the ambulance."

That word *moment* lodged itself somewhere in me, small and useless.

Then he exhaled.

"But we couldn't bring her back."

I didn't move. The doctor kept talking—formal phrases, gentle wording, maybe my name, but it all slid past me without meaning.

All I could visualize in that moment was her body—lying still in a way that didn't belong to the living—seared into my retinas like a bad tattoo I'd never chosen.

That's all it took to rewrite everything.

From that point on, I lived in a world with no path back.

And somehow the world around me didn't react. The walls stood where they always had. The streetlights kept their constant glow. People walked past without pausing. Everything carried on, aloof, like death hadn't just walked through my life and taken what it came for.

I'VE GOT A WAR IN MY MIND

The house held its stillness with an unnerving grip. Every room felt paused, as if the moment I lost her had settled into the walls and refused to loosen. I walked the length of the living room, stopping where my knees had hit the floor the night before, and lowered myself onto the wood, cool against my palms, and sat there with my back against the sofa.

My hands shook as I pulled my knees to my chest, trying to take up less space, less air, less everything. If I got small enough, the sadness would miss me.

But it didn't. It settled in, and from there, it spread.

The morning after she died, I called my childhood friend Nicole—not Pier One Nicole, but hometown Nicole, the one whom my mom adored. Mom had a soft spot for Nicole from the beginning of our friendship. She'd glance at her with this proud, amused smile and say she looked "straight off a cereal box." To mom, that meant something specific—wholesome in that unmistakably girl-next-door way, an all-American pretty that didn't need the effort of explanation.

She answered on the first ring, her voice solid in that familiar way that always made my mom light up. When I told her what happened, there was a brief pause—tears—one heartbeat, and then "I'm coming." No hesitation. No questions.

By that afternoon, she had packed her SUV, left her own world behind, and started the three-plus-hour drive to South Georgia, heading straight into the place I couldn't bear to face alone.

I moved through the house slower than I meant to, tracing the spots where her things still lived, untouched. Her handwriting kept appearing in places I didn't expect—smooth loops on an index card, a grocery list tucked behind a notebook, a sticky note on the fridge in her favorite pen. I couldn't bring myself to read them, but the idea of throwing them out felt impossible.

I took the frames off the walls one by one and set them on the dining table. Dishes mom loved went into sheets of yesterday's newspaper, the ink smudging my fingers as I folded each corner. Piece by piece, her world slid into plastic bins lined up across the living room. I kept arranging them, lining them up in rows, telling myself it would make the grief feel contained if I could just get everything in order.

No one warns you how mourning rewires you—how you

become equal parts guardian and collector, trying to hold on to pieces of someone you can't touch anymore.

I told myself that having a task might quiet the ache for a moment. But boxing up her things didn't touch the part of me that was breaking. Even once I cleared the counters and the shelves were bare, sadness still lived in the corners she used to fill with laughter.

In her closet, her favorite shirts still carried the faintest trace of her perfume. I'd lift one from the hanger and lean in, letting that warm, floral scent rise—so familiar it felt like she might speak from behind me. I knew exactly what it would do to me, but I pressed my face into the fabric anyway, holding on to the only version of her I could still reach.

My body felt foreign, as if every emotion had bypassed whatever defenses I once had. They arrived in full force, no warning, no buffer, leaving me exposed to all of it. Even the bathroom mirror became a kind of reckoning. I'd lift my toothbrush, pause mid-motion, and study the tired version of myself staring back—trying to place the day, the hour, anything that would cement me to the present.

Light from the vanity poured over me with no mercy, flattening every part of the room into high definition. Colors rose too bright, details too crisp—nothing agreed to soften or fade into the background.

Everything around me kept functioning with absolute certainty—while I struggled to remember how to move through any of it. The ceiling fan was smug about spinning around with mechanical purpose, indifferent to the fact that I was unraveling beneath it. Even the side table in the hallway seemed positioned to watch me, its surface cleared, waiting, as though the house itself expected something from me I couldn't give.

At night, I buried my face in the pillow, screaming until the sound drained out of me, because closing my eyes was worse. That's when everything I was trying not to see came back in perfect detail.

The moment my eyes closed, I was back in her living room—next to my mom's body on the floor. The worst moment of my life became my mind's favorite re-run. And somehow I was both the star and the unwilling audience, trapped in an endless Sundance submission with zero plot and way too much trauma.

Grief left me stranded somewhere unfamiliar. No signs. No shoulder to pull over to. Just heat rising off the asphalt and the sinking sense that I'd missed the last good exit miles ago. Parts of me were scattered across the road—glass, metal, smoke—from places I hadn't even known were on fire.

I kept waiting for a sign. Like a literal one. Preferably neon. Something subtle, like: *YOU'RE FUCKED. MERGE LEFT.*

That's when I began pulling bricks from my own foundation, like a house slowly collapsing on purpose—zero permits and a deep commitment to poor decisions. No plan.

I didn't pace myself. Just complete demolition—ripping out support beams and lighting the match, then acting surprised when it caught on fire. I left it there, the way I left my own potential—untouched, gathering dust, easier to abandon than to save.

There were times I'd slipped out of the world before—when my mom was in the hospital, or during those swept under the rug, invisible battles no one knew I was fighting. I'd go quiet, duck out of plans, let texts or calls sit unanswered.

But those earlier disappearances felt temporary, recoverable. I'd always snapped back eventually—loud, busy, full of motion, like I hadn't just gone missing.

This time, I stayed gone. I *just* snapped.

I couldn't stay in Leesburg. Atlanta felt far enough away to breathe, so I crashed at Lola's for a few days—the childhood friend who once catfished me and tried to drag me out of the closet.

Nothing in my world had changed, but being beside someone who actually knew me, on streets that once held ordinary memories, gave the day a small sense of footing. The city didn't heal anything, but it softened the freefall.

Lola's loft carried its usual mix of exposed brick, tall windows, and echo—nothing soft to catch sound, nothing to hide inside. "Rosemary" by Deftones played low through her speakers, drifting through the open space while she swept the last few strands of my hair from a haircut she'd given me into a small pile near her chair.

The eucalyptus from her candle still lingered near the kitchen, a calm that didn't match the tempest building in my chest. I took a few steps toward the couch, trying to settle myself in the open stretch of her loft, when something inside me gave out mid-stride.

My back found the wall, legs weakening beneath the weight of whatever hit. The sound ripped free before I even knew I was breathing. It tore through my throat and shot across the loft, hitting the brick and all those tall windows with a force that didn't feel human.

Lola's voice barely reached me. Then her hand found my back, warm through the fabric of my shirt. The room around us stretched in every direction—brick, glass, open floors; it felt like grief could echo forever in a place that big. But she stayed there, knees bent, palm resting between my shoulder blades, anchoring me to something real when I had lost every sense of where my body ended.

"Trey..." Her voice was barely above a whisper. "Eighteen years. That's how long we've been in each other's lives." She paused, swallowing hard, her eyes misting before the words made it out. "I knew your mom. I knew how she looked at you. There was nothing in her world she loved more."

She brushed her thumb under my eye to wipe away my tears. Her hand rose slowly, almost hesitantly, before her thumb traced beneath my eye. She caught the tear before it could fall, "And I love you too," she said, "Seeing you here... like this." She stopped, wiped a tear from her own eye, "It's breaking something in me."

I shook my head, barely able to form words.

"I...I can't believe this hap...pened. W...why did it have to happen like this?" My voice cracked. "She's gone. She's not coming back."

My forehead rested against my knees when Lola's hand slid into mine. I looked back up, and she was already watching me with that familiar, no-nonsense focus she saved for the people she loved.

"Hey," she said, voice dipping lower, but sure of itself. "You know I'd show up for you in any way you need."

Something flickered across her face then—an idea forming in real time. She squeezed my hand once more, then eased her fingers free.

"Stay here," she murmured, already rising to her feet. "I think I have something that can help you."

I curled into myself again, forehead pressed to my arms, everything folded tight across my knees. My breath hit the floor in uneven bursts; I couldn't even get my face high enough to see her, only the blurred grain in the floorboards beneath me.

"Trey," she said from above me, calm but firm. "Hold out your arm. Open your hand."

I still didn't lift my head. I didn't ask. I just loosened my grip around my knees and extended my arm toward the sound of her voice, palm open, trembling.

I thought I was waiting for something small, a cool shape settling into the center of my hand.

A pill.

Relief.

Something to take the spikes out of my chest.

Xanax, I thought. That had to be it.

"Now make a fist."

Something brushed my upper arm—a quick tug, fabric pulled through a loop, drawn firm around my bicep. A scarf, maybe. Or a bandana. I couldn't tell.

I heard her move, fast and focused.

Then the needle touched me.

A small pinch, nothing more, swallowed instantly by the rawness already burning behind my eyes.

The loft stayed still—brick, windows, open floors, yet my body slid into a softness I didn't recognize. It spread fast. Too fast, rushing through my veins with a heat that didn't belong to me.

Muscles that had been clenched for days loosened at once, providing a strange calm that didn't belong to grief or shock. My arms fell away from my knees, and my breath slipped out in one long exhale I couldn't control.

A single question lit up in my mind, then split into more, each one tumbling over the next:

What did she put in me?

Why is my body sinking?

Why can't I move the way I want to?

Part of me knew something was wrong.

Another part didn't care.

That second part grew fast with the sweeping relief that felt both unreal and dangerously welcome.

She crouched in front of me, caught my drifting focus, and said it plainly, leaving no room for misunderstanding:

I'd been injected with heroin.

When I opened my eyes the next morning, my mind felt scattered across the room. Memory tried to pull itself together, but the pieces didn't match—scenes blinked in and out, half-formed and strange; spliced in moments from a dream I hadn't meant to enter. But nothing settled long enough for me to trust it.

One stretch of the night stayed intact, though.

I remembered the highway.

The rush of passing lights.

Lola's hand was steady on the wheel.

My arm hangs out the window, fingers spreading and tracing the wind.

We pulled into a driveway I recognized only by the shape of the house—Nicole's. I didn't get out. My body stayed slumped against the passenger door, head tilted toward the open window.

Nicole came straight to me, leaning down until her face filled the frame of the window. Her mouth moved—words I couldn't catch—and I tried to respond, but my tongue felt slack, too heavy to assemble a sentence. If anything made it out, it wasn't language.

Lola answered for me, calmly and too smoothly, telling Nicole I was drunk. A perfect explanation meant to close the door on any real questions, especially the ones that might point back to her.

I'd crossed a line and not blurred it, not tiptoed near it, crossed it.

It didn't feel like "casual experimentation" people chalk up to being in your twenties: party drugs, ecstasy at a festival, or a bump in a bathroom stall at a club. This was heroin. I never thought I'd be in the same room with it, let alone have it in my body. Not my scene—it was *Requiem for a Dream*.

Lola had watched me unravel and watched me come apart in real time. And instead of holding me up, she took the opening. Slipped a needle into my arm without hesitation, like it was medicine. Like, my consent was irrelevant. Like I was already too far gone to notice or care. Like I was her.

Less than a month earlier, I'd stood over a cake, candles flickering, my mom laughing somewhere behind me. Life had borders then—clear ones. Days felt solid, predictable in a way ordinary life tricks you into thinking it's permanent. I still believed in routines, in tomorrow, in the simple safety of "before."

And now, *this*.

When had she slipped into heroin?

And when had I stopped seeing the signs?

Nothing arrived in a clean line—just small flashes that finally made sense when I looked back. Lola's hands were trembling when she thought my eyes were elsewhere. That dullness in her voice that used to have dimension. Long paused where her charm once lived. And the quiet she'd sink into—not the restful kind at all, her body waiting for another dose before drowsiness overtook her.

Pieces I'd brushed off at the time.

Pieces that spelled out a truth I hadn't wanted to read.

What she did was reckless; there's no softening that. And as fucked up as it was, it didn't come from cruelty. It came from a frantic kind of need that grows as someone sinks, grabbing whatever is closest just to stay afloat. In her mind, pulling me into that moment was her connection—even if it meant dragging me into the same dark water she was fighting.

After that night, I shoved the memory—and whatever was left of our friendship—into a locked room in my mind and walked away from it. I couldn't face it, couldn't even brush against the edges without feeling the ground crumble beneath me. There were already too many crises burning at once, too

many parts of my life demanding attention. I told myself I'd deal with it later, once the smoke cleared.

Something in me understood the truth long before I said it out loud. That night had teeth. It showed me exactly how fast life can spiral into something unrecognizable. Whatever rush tore through me that night wasn't a door I could walk back through. It was a warning—crystal clear.

I saw the danger for what it was, not in theory, but in my own veins. And it only took one misstep to understand I wouldn't survive crossing it again.

Mother's Day 2013 didn't tap me on the shoulder; it hit straight through me, stealing whatever breath I had left. I was back in Leesburg by then, moving through my mom's house alone, pretending I could function at Pier One while waiting for the For Sale sign in the yard to decide my fate, then crawl back to Atlanta with whatever remained of me.

The store was dressed as if nothing had happened—pastel banners curled overhead, cheering, "Happy Mother's Day!" in curly letters that looked one tantrum away from sprouting wings. Towers of ceramic vases and pointless throw pillows stood arranged with the sort of enthusiasm only a corporate display team could muster.

Every cheerful setup felt personally offensive—like the décor had teamed up to knee me square in the balls then applaud itself for the effort. I'd stand under those pastel "Happy Mother's Day!" signs with my jaw clenched so tight it could have cracked a tile, staring straight through the cheerful lettering. The same thought kept barreling through me with zero subtlety:

Why the fuck does everyone else still get a mom?

Customers floated in with their chipper little voices and Target-commercial attitudes, tossing small talk around like confetti I never asked to be a part of. Every question they lobbed at me scraped across my nerves with the enthusiasm of the key that totaled my car senior year.

Then came Pillow Lady.

"I don't know if this rug matches the pillows," she squeaked, like she was auditioning for a Disney side character. "Do you think these yellows clash?" She pointed left. "This one gives me sunburned-chick vibes," then right, "and this is *definitely* lemon zest."

I stared at the wall of pillows behind her—floor to ceiling, arranged by color with cult-level precision—and for a split second, I pictured climbing to the very top just to swan-dive off and put us both out of our misery.

Instead of chucking myself off the pillow wall, I reached into my pocket, found the Xanax I kept there, and snapped it in half with my thumb. The piece dissolved under my tongue while Pillow Lady kept rambling about citrus-themed décor.

By that point, every shift began with that same small blue pill—prescribed and blessed by whatever merciful doctor decided I shouldn't be left unsupervised with my own emotions. It didn't fix anything, but it got me just functional enough to ring up whatever nonsense people hauled to the register, nod politely, and avoid having a public meltdown in the oil-diffuser aisle.

Even hearing someone clear their throat in my direction made my entire body tense, bracing for that one question I couldn't stomach: *How are you?*

What was I supposed to say?

That I felt erased?

That whatever version of me used to exist had been crossed out sentence by sentence until I was basically a public-facing government document—pages of black bars and one lonely noun trying its best to survive?

LANDSLIDE IN SKINNY JEANS

I'd built a decent circle of friends in Leesburg—good people, generous in the ways that matter—but they didn't carry the history I needed. Not then. I needed someone who could read me without translation. Someone who remembered the version of me that laughed without effort, before everything caved in.

I didn't want new.

I wanted familiar.

I wanted the kind of company where I didn't have to explain a single thing for it to make sense.

I needed Atlanta.

And no shade to the genuinely kind people I met in Leesburg, but I'd exceeded my limit. Every conversation circled back to backyard smokers, small-town scandal, or how the new Publix

compares to the old Piggly Wiggly. None of it fed anything in me except the urge to drive north and never look back.

I had to get out of South Georgia.

More urgently, I had to get out of that house.

Being there felt wrong in a way I couldn't fix—too still, too preserved. It felt like being entombed in a mausoleum with no door.

By the time my mom's house sold, I needed a job lined up in Atlanta, so when I wasn't knee-deep in throw pillows or slicing open another shipment of ceramic roosters, I was chained to my laptop—scrolling LinkedIn, refreshing career pages, diving into job boards...triaging my own life.

I cast the net wide: marketing, sales, anything that even vaguely resembled my lane. I had the degree, the experience, the drive. On paper, I looked solid.

I'd refresh job boards the way people swipe dating apps— hoping the perfect match would suddenly appear, even though I'd already seen and applied to every sad, mismatched listing three times that day.

After a while, the posts all blended into one long, disappointing chant. Some font, same corporate optimism, exact requirements:

The ideal candidate has just enough experience to make you doubt your entire résumé. Must be charming but not too energetic. Confident but never threatening. Flexible but also laser-focused—a self-starter who simultaneously thrives under constant supervision.

It was like applying to be a pilot with a master's degree in Greek. I'd never fit the bill.

Even my close friend, Forkel, the one from college, stepped in. She'd been in my life long enough to recognize when I was circling the drain but still pretending I was fine.

Without telling me, she hired a résumé writer on my behalf after my job search stalled. It slipped past both my pride and my overdrawn bank account in one clean move. It was the quiet, practical rescue I never knew how to ask for.

But no amount of help could change where I was. My mind felt like a climb I wasn't trained for—steep, raw, and unpredictable. The worst had already come and gone, and once you've lived through that kind of loss, the rest of the world loses its threat. There was nothing left that anyone could take from me that would come close.

Inside that hollow space, something unexpected materialized: a violent sort of freedom. The kind that only shows up after everything explodes. I kept picturing myself barefoot at ground zero, the blast long over, debris drifting around me, and somehow I was still upright. Still breathing. Still here.

In the debris, pieces of my life glimmered through—damaged, leaking sorrow into each other until nothing felt distinct. It all lay around me in pieces, shards of the life I'd been trying to hold together.

None of it made sense.

A scrap of the years I spent bending myself into shapes I thought might finally make me "normal" for my family. Another piece showing the truth—yet no amount of pretending ever closed the gap, and coming out twice only widened it.

A fragment of the smile I used as a cover while two parts of me pulled in opposite directions: faith tugging one way, sexuality tugging back, leaving me stuck somewhere in the middle, exhausted from trying to hold both.

My mom's illness was everywhere, intertwined with every decision we made. Even the tiny ones. Especially the tiny ones. It dictated the cadence of our house, the future, and the parts of myself I'd get to grow into one day.

Off to the side, half-buried beneath everything else, was the piece I always pretended didn't cut—my father's absence. Not an accident. A choice. One I'd taught myself to swallow long before I dared to admit any of it hurt.

Layered over all of it, I lost my mom in a way that rewrote me. Suddenly, not peaceful, not distant. I was there. I saw everything and nothing in my life had felt the same since.

No way to pick one piece up without feeling all of them.

I always expected to be ready when it happened—when my mom passed. She spent so many years teetering on the edge that I convinced myself the real thing would somehow be less painful. I told myself I'd built up calluses from all the close calls. That I'd have a go-bag and playlist ready—some curated mix title *In Case the Worst Finally Happens,* featuring Bon Iver and one tasteful hymn.

Turns out that none of that was true.

When it happened for real, my mind just...emptied.

Everything inside me rushed out at once, the way a drawer spills its contents when someone pulls too hard, too fast.

There's no preparing for a moment like that. No handbook. No emotional checklist. No gentle easing-in.

I started drinking the night she went to the hospital, and after she was gone, I never really found the brakes. One night blurred into the next—a drink, vodka soda in my hand before I even realized I'd made it. When it wasn't alcohol, it was weed.

I remember whole nights where I'd get high and let my body take over before my thoughts could ruin the moment. One hit from the bong, then another, and the living room stopped feeling like a tomb and turned into the closest thing I had to escape. Music blasting, lights low, and me— barefoot, loose, moving hard enough to outrun the heaviness for a while.

And every night, one song always elbowed its way to the front.

"We Can't Stop" by Miley Cyrus.

It started as a random shuffle. Then it became a ritual. I'd replay it on a loop—dancing like someone had cut the strings holding me up, jumping across the floor with zero choreography and even less shame.

That song gave me a break from drowning.

When my mom's house finally sold that summer, my sister and I split the remaining estate. After the bills, paperwork, and all the costs—the aftereffects of death that no one warns you about—it wasn't much. Just enough to press my foot on the gas and not look back.

I kept feeding myself the same promise: Atlanta would fix me. Not the actual city, the idea of it. The skyline I'd memorized years earlier. The way it rose from the highway, all glass and gridlock, sure of itself in a way I hadn't been in

months. I convinced myself that if I could just get back there, the version of me I used to know would be waiting.

In my mind, it was medicine. The cure. The reboot. The clean slate I insisted was waiting somewhere past exit 247. I'd find my footing, land a real job, and slip back into my life like nothing had shattered—like grief could be undone with a fresh LinkedIn bio and access to restaurants boasting fancier cuisine than just mozzarella sticks and spinach artichoke dip.

Not that I was eating. By the time I packed everything I owned into a U-Haul and my SUV that August, I'd dropped nearly twenty pounds since my mom died. And it wasn't like I'd started with much—one-forty at five-nine barely gave me cushion to lose.

I moved into the cheapest apartment I could afford, tucked off Deering Road, so that I could be near my best friend Jessica. The place marketed itself as "luxury," though the bar for that title was clearly on the floor. The leasing office bragged about *amenities*—which, from what I could tell, meant the building still had a roof and most of the doors locked if you jiggled them first.

The gym was their crown jewel. A single rusty Huffy bike leaned on cinder blocks in the corner, looking exhausted from simply existing. The treadmill beside it had a belt that had given up sometime around the recession; stepping on it felt like a trust fall with no catcher.

But my new *luxury* apartment wasn't in South Georgia. And it was mine. For all its moldy corners and suspicious plumbing, I was grateful. Grateful to be out. To be near someone who knew the unabridged version of me. Appreciative of all four walls and a roof—however questionably attached—that didn't come with ghosts or grief baked into the floorboards.

Being with friends gave me these brief pockets of relief, little windows where the world loosened its grip. Two drinks in, and I could almost slip back into the version of myself I'd been before everything detonated. For an hour or so, it felt like Atlanta hadn't changed, like my mom was only a few hours away down the highway. I could almost pass for the person I used to be.

But once I crossed a certain threshold, I'd come apart in dramatic, high-definition fashion.

Going out stopped being social; it became a mission. One goal: blackout as fast as humanly possible. A complete emotional landslide in skinny jeans. The kind of mess friends scooped off bathroom tiles with the reflexes of EMTs, explaining to concerned strangers, "He's just going through some stuff," petting my back the way you comfort a newly adopted rescue dog during its first thunderstorm.

Apparently, there was one night when I'd already blasted past my limit, when a group of about ten of us left the bar and started the walk back to Jessica's. I drifted ahead of the group, not paying attention, and stepped straight into the street. A car barreled toward me, brakes screaming, horn blaring. The driver yelled something I definitely earned.

According to my friends, I didn't like that he yelled at me, so stepped up to his hood and slammed my fist down on it. Hard.

Then they told me the driver got out.

He stepped toward me with a gun in his hand, asking

if I wanted to "hit his fucking car again." My friends said they were screaming at me, trying to pull me back, trying to talk him down. I was too drunk to register any of it. Too far gone to know what I was, seconds away from disappearing from this earth because I got blackout and belligerent on a random Tuesday.

I didn't remember a second of it.

Not the horn. Not the gun. Not the fear on my friends' faces.

Another morning, I came with my sheets and T-shirt soaked through—dark, tacky, everywhere. A few disoriented moments—I honestly thought I was dreaming. Then I pushed myself upright. At the bend of my right arm was an open gash, deep enough that pale tissue showed through. I shot down the hall to Jessica's room and shook her awake before I even found words.

Neither one of us had any idea how it happened. We just kept looking from the wound to each other, as if one of us might suddenly remember, "Oh right, that's when you tried to backflip in the bathroom." But we had nothing.

I didn't have insurance, so we patched my arm up ourselves—antiseptic that burned like hell, butterfly closures that lined up with the precision of two amateurs pretending we knew what we were doing, and towels we didn't bother saving.

It wasn't until later that the story filled itself in, piece by piece, from the bartender and half a dozen people who'd seen the whole thing unfold.

I'd climbed onto the bar, moving with the music, slipping,

losing my balance—and then I went down hard, arm first. They said the impact was loud enough to be heard, even over the music. And then the blood came.

I was bleeding so much the staff had to raid the bar's first-aid kit, wrapping my arm in gauze and tape just to get me out the door. I didn't remember any of it.

All I had was the aftermath: that makeshift bandage twisted into the knot of my sheets when I did laundry, stiff with dried blood and fused to the fabric like part of the bedding. What was left behind would eventually heal into a raised mark on my arm, a permanent reminder of how far off the rails I slid.

Friends approached me as if I were glass. They were careful in the way people get when they want to help but have no damn idea where to start. There's no syllabus for grief, no choreography that tells you where to put your hands or how close to stand.

What stayed with me wasn't anything they said; it was how they showed up—sitting beside me on porch steps long after the sun dipped out. Driving me around for no reason except that motion felt easier than stillness. Pulling up outside my apartment after another job rejection. No pep talks. Just people who refused to let me sit alone in whatever version showed up that day.

But even packed into a bar—music thumping, shoulders brushing mine—I felt removed from it all, sealed off behind something invisible and soundproof.

Everyone else kept moving forward without hesitation: engagements announced over mimosas, promotions toasted

with bottom-shelf champagne, new houses with granite they were all too proud of.

Their lives expanded. Meanwhile, mine stayed locked in a room I couldn't seem to find the door to. They never saw the part after the bartenders dimmed the lights. The nights I couldn't lift myself off the floor, when even breathing felt optional. And how could they? I didn't let anyone get close enough.

Except for one person.

EVERYBODY KNEW THAT WE HAD TOO MUCH FUN

Jessica and I share the kind of bond that feels older than both of us, like we've been circling each other across lifetimes just to land here together.

In 2018, I had one of those dreams that don't feel like dreams, more like memories you haven't lived yet.

In my dream, Jessica was pregnant with her second child, and I knew—without anyone saying it—that the baby was a girl. The color, the light, even the way she held her belly...it all felt startlingly real.

When I woke up, the dream clung to me, bright and insistent—just like a sticky note slapped to the front of my brain. I sat on the edge of my bed, rubbed my eyes, and typed a quick email to myself: *Call Jess about the dream.*

Later that morning, I phoned her.

"Okay, this is going to sound nuts," I said, "But I had this insanely vivid dream last night. You were pregnant...and it was a girl."

She paused. There was this tiny hitch in her breath—barely a second, but enough for me to hear something deeper on her end of the line.

"That's...wild," she said. "Actually...really crazy shit."

And then, just as fast, she swerved lanes. "Anyway—did I tell you what happened at the spa the other day...?"

Then we hung up, and the conversation folded itself neatly into the rest of the morning...nothing unusual.

The next day, my phone lights up—Jessica. No hesitation. I answered.

"Hey," she says, voice a little softer than usual. "You got a sec?"

There's a pause, one of those loaded, careful silences where you can feel someone reaching for the right place to start.

"So...about that dream you told me yesterday..." she said slowly.

"You're not going to believe this. I didn't really know what to say at the time—I was kind of in shock."

I didn't say anything. I could feel my breath climbing up into my throat.

"I *am* pregnant," she says. "Twelve weeks today." We don't know the gender yet...but that's wild.

About a month later, she sends a text: *It's a girl.*

I reply: *lol, yeah—I know.*

Even now, that story gives me chills.

That's the kind of connection we have. We met in sixth grade and never really let go.

Our ears didn't need the words—our eyes always did the talking. Those looks we'd toss across a bar or through the blur of a festival crowd said everything louder than any conversation could. Looks where your whole face shifts, where you don't just smile—you *recognize* each other.

Jessica knew me better than anyone. Not because we tried for it, but because it was baked into us—years of inside jokes, late-night drives with windows down, photos of us grinning so hard our faces looked like they might crack. Everybody knew that we had too much fun, we'd walk into places all lit up, bright—cheeks flushed—moving as a unit, no daylight between us.

She saw every version of me: the loud one, the reckless one, the soft one buried under everything I didn't say out loud. She knew the parts of me that broke first and the parts to rebuild slowly. And for the first time outside of my relationship with my mom or sister, I realized someone loved me for who I actually was—not just the version that cracked jokes, hosted the room, or made everybody feel taken care of.

She loved the real thing.

The whole messy, complicated thing.

Except Jessica didn't know all of it.

It's not that I didn't trust her, or that she'd judge me. I trusted her with my life. I didn't want her to know the worst of it because I couldn't bear the look on her face if she knew just how far I was slipping in my first eight weeks back in

Atlanta. If she saw it—really saw it—I might not come back from that.

In my mid-twenties, I'd messed around with party drugs the way people try on sunglasses at a mall kiosk—briefly, carelessly, with zero attachment. Fun when it happened, forgettable when it didn't. Nothing I ever chased. Nothing I ever "needed."

No one blinked if you did a couple of lines on a Friday or Saturday. What no one knew was that for me, Friday and Saturday never ended. Cocaine gave me something that felt close enough to a baseline that I stopped questioning it. I could stand upright in my own life again, crack a joke, make eye contact, and not break down in tears.

For about eight weeks, I fell in with a small pocket of people I kept completely separate from everyone who actually knew me. They were hurting too—not in the same ways I was, but enough that we recognized the darkness in each other. And they were always wired, always chasing the next surge, the next hour awake.

Very quickly, I wasn't myself anymore. I was doing things I would've sworn, even a few months earlier, were impossible for me. My heart was in pieces, and the moral clarity my mom instilled in me in those days felt like something I'd kept in a storage unit. I could sometimes hear her voice in the background, faint, like it was coming through a bathroom vent. And I ignored it every time.

Once I let myself slip, really slip, it was like stepping into a current too strong to fight. I stopped asking who I was becoming. I just opened the door, let the darkness rush in, and let the night decide what happened next. I had no bearings.

The first break in the storm happened sometime in early November; it wasn't some elaborate, cinematic dream. I was back in my childhood home, sitting across from my mom like it was any ordinary afternoon. No big moment, no glowing light, no dramatic reunion. Just her. Present. Alive.

She didn't say much—just my name, the way she used to when she'd catch the truth in my face long before I was ready to speak it.

And the second she said it—*Trey...*

It felt like she was moving through me, page by page, taking in every reckless turn I'd taken: the drinking, the drugs, the nights I tried to outrun myself. It felt like she was holding a mirror to my face, and for the first time, I couldn't look away.

She wasn't angry.

She had a look that said, *Baby, I know exactly what you're doing to yourself.*

Suddenly I could see it—clearer than anything I'd felt since she died.

Two paths.

One was the one I was already on: numbing myself into the ground, reducing my world to bars, powder, and blackout nights. A path that ended short and dark.

The other was the one she would've wanted for me— the one that didn't waste the life she fought her whole life to give me.

Neither road was scenic. One ended in a parking lot

behind a bar with more than just a shoe missing and a tab of drinks I didn't remember ordering—the other—unclear. But at least it didn't come with an overdose or an addiction I couldn't walk away from.

In that dream, sitting across from her, I understood something I'd been refusing to admit.

No one was coming to save me.

But I still had a choice.

And I wasn't about to choose the path that made her watch me disappear.

That night, I'm convinced it was God—and my mom—reaching me in the only way I'd actually listen. It showed up as a dream, sure, but it didn't feel like one. I felt awake. Exposed. Terrified. I had no idea how to pull my life back together. I felt ashamed of how far I'd let myself slip, how easily I kept excusing the next bad choice with, *Well, I've already done all this shit...what does one more matter?*

But underneath all that shame was something else too... luck. Because honestly, I didn't know how I was still alive.

I just knew things couldn't stay the same.

The first change happened when Jess invited me to move into her townhouse—quietly handing me something I hadn't felt in months: stability. She didn't make a speech or ask for anything in return; her offer itself said everything: *You don't have to do this alone.*

In the middle of all that wreckage, she reminded me love hadn't vanished; it had just changed shape. She saw something worth salvaging when I couldn't see past the ruin. Especially then.

It had only been four weeks. The hard drugs were gone, and I was still figuring out what to do with the drinking. By the time December rolled into Atlanta, the air had the crisp, undecided chill—caught somewhere between fall and winter. Cold enough to make me tug my jacket closer, even for the thirty-second walk from the car.

Mostly, I was just relieved the worst year of my life was finally limping toward its end.

Somehow, in the middle of all that carnage, I was excited...

I was going on a date.

I'm annoyingly punctual—the guy who shows up early and then pretends he just got there. But that night, I made a conscious choice to be five minutes late. Just five. Fashionably late, not rude.

I couldn't explain it then; I think I needed that tiny illusion of control. A first date after the year I'd had, maybe I just wanted to feel like I wasn't showing up desperate or too eager. Perhaps I needed to believe I was stepping into this new thing on my own terms—even if all I did was sit in my car for a few extra minutes, watching my breath fog up the windshield.

When I "pulled in" the parking lot, I shot him a text. His name was Michael, and I figured I should at least pretend I was only *slightly* behind schedule. So I told him I'd just arrived and added, *"You can't miss me—I'll be the one walking in wearing a feather boa."*

A stupid joke. Pure me. Typically, the sort of humor that sits for a second too long before the other person decides whether I'm serious.

But Michael didn't hesitate. Not even a beat.

"Perfect," he replied. *"I'm sure it'll complement my assless chaps nicely."*

And something about that—the speed, the confidence, the matching ridiculousness—hit me in a place I wasn't used to being met. It felt like someone finally spoke my language back to me without needing a translation.

From the parking lot, the place barely announced itself—tucked between an art supply shop and a salon. You could drive past a hundred times without realizing it served anything more special than takeout.

But once I stepped inside, the whole mood changed.

Tuk Tuk opened up like a two-story lantern...warm, gold-toned, and full of subtle detail. The lighting hovered in that in-between space that made faces look easier to read, conversations easier to start. Tables sat under a side ceiling threaded with tiny bulbs that gave the room a calm, almost festive glow.

Michael was already seated when I walked in—settled in that calm way people have when they're not performing for anyone. His head scanned the menu, hands relaxed, no phone to hide behind, no nervous shifting, as if the seat had been waiting for him.

He rose when he saw me.

And the moment our eyes met, something flickered inside the room: sound, color, awareness—all of it coming back into focus. His blue eyes held mine with a directness that didn't push or rush, just certainty, like he'd already decided I wasn't a stranger.

RECALCULATING ROUTE...

Grief doesn't come with an instruction manual. No blinking "You Are Here" dot, no GPS voice calmly instructing, "In 300 feet, turn left toward healing." And even if it did, I'd still end up lost—because I am the kind of person who gets turned around leaving a parking garage. I'd insist I knew a shortcut, ignore the map entirely, and wind up ugly crying while GPS recalculated for the fifth time. Still somehow holding out for a hopeful sign that says, "Next exit: Closure," like that was ever on my route.

Grief kicks in the door like it's on a trashy reality show, flips your furniture, raids your fridge, and leaves its dirty socks on your coffee table. It lives rent-free, and somehow convinces you to carry its crap everywhere you go. Like it's your job, and

just when you think it might finally leave, it clogs the toilet and steals your phone charger.

I thought I could ghost grief—slip out a side door and pretend I never lived there. But it tailed me everywhere. Into every bar. Into every conversation. It kept close enough to steer me toward whatever numbed the quickest. I'd lift a glass I didn't care about, knock back whatever made contact with my hand, and wait for the blackout to do the cleanup.

Turns out, you can't outrun something that's already free-loading in your head.

Truthfully, the year before I moved to South Georgia, I wasn't exactly operating from my highest wisdom. I kept making choices that chipped away at whatever structure I had left. The move would be a reset, a chance for me to rebuild, to get my footing finally.

But right as I started piecing things together, my mom died, and everything I was holding came apart. It was nuclear.

Those two tracks, the unraveling and the loss, collided so cleanly it felt engineered.

Alcohol wasn't new to me. It was already in my bloodline, already a presence in my house long before I picked up a glass. My mom's dad was twenty-nine when he missed a turn and drove straight through someone's front wall. He was drunk. He died instantly.

My sister and I didn't grow up around healthy boundaries with alcohol. In our house, drinking was the kind of thing everyone pretended wasn't the truth at all. The Wild Turkey lived in a metal flask that never stayed full for long. The vodka hid between the mattress and the box spring. Cups insisted they held grapefruit juice, even when the smell burned before the first sip.

Nothing stayed hidden, not the scent, not the moods, not the sudden storms. I just assumed that's what alcohol did to people: turned adults into versions of themselves you avoided until the room settled again. It never crossed my mind that something deeper might be unraveling underneath it all.

I tried alcohol in high school, sure—but it wasn't a habit. It was whatever someone's older sibling could get their hands on, usually Zima or Smirnoff Ice, the starter pack for suburban teen rebellion. I'd drink only if there were a couch or a basement to crash in. It never followed me home.

It felt fun, but also weirdly loaded. Each sip skimmed the surface of a pattern I'd watched my whole life, a pattern that had already taken things from me well before I ever lifted a bottle.

After that, I was scared. From seventeen to twenty-four, I didn't touch alcohol or drugs. They were hazard signs blinking: "Don't go there." I didn't see them as a good time—I saw everything I wanted to forget, or not become lined up like mile markers.

I spent years trying to seal off the mess—nailing boards over the parts of myself I didn't want to feed. I told myself I was breaking the cycle. Really, I was just renovating a haunted house and hiding the ghosts behind fresh drywall. And by the time I finally stopped to look around, I realized I wasn't outrunning the past at all.

I learned to speak it.

But I had a new motivation. After more than a year of

throwing résumés into the void, I finally got the call. February 2014. Initiative—an ad agency in Atlanta under the IPG network—wanted me.

Joe, the general manager, and Melody, his right hand, saw something in me I hadn't seen in a year. Maybe longer. They sifted past the shaky confidence, the gaps, the pieces I'd been taping together just to keep going. Somehow, they saw potential instead of damage.

That moment rerouted everything. I still had a future to claim—one I hadn't ruined, one that was still waiting on me to step back into it.

I was the oldest assistant there—almost seven years senior to the bright-eyed, fresh-out-of-college hires still pretending they liked LaCroix. My bank account was in witness protection. I was so broke I'd pour end-of-the-day office coffee, let it go cold on the ride home, and reheat it the next morning, and it felt like it was a luxury.

But I didn't care. I had health insurance. Direct deposit and payments that didn't bounce. And structure. Real structure.

Also...Michael and I were dating.

We were still learning each other—careful, cautious, almost in slow motion. Some days it felt less like a relationship and more like two people trying to rebuild something while still standing in the debris. We both knew one wrong move could reopen things we were barely beginning to understand.

In 2013, we'd both come undone—knocked sideways in completely different ways. Through all that trauma, we still found ourselves in the same place at the same time.

One of the first things I noticed about Michael is how easily he settled into any space. He didn't need attention. He didn't need managing. He enjoyed people. He just arrived, comfortable in his skin in a way I hadn't experienced in a relationship.

That mattered to me more than I could articulate then...

Because I am social. Loud. Expressive. I love people, energy, and conversation. And for years, that part of me had been handled like a liability, something to tone down, something that took up too much room.

With Michael, there was no need to shrink. I didn't have to dim anything for him to feel comfortable beside.

It wasn't quite a love story—not then. It was two people recognizing damage in each other and choosing not to look away.

The real transformation hadn't started yet.

GUATEMALA

I landed in Guatemala thinking I was there to offer something—to fix, to serve, to balance the scale after the carnage I'd left behind. But what waited for me was nothing I could have scripted. I didn't know it then, but some part of me had been bracing for this, somewhere that could show me how to see again, with clearer eyes.

I learned what *nothing* really looked like. Not the kind of 'unfair' we gripe about over a $9 latte, while someone else survives on less than $2 a day. Actual nothing—I saw homes patched together with rusted sheet metal, tarp edges nailed straight into concrete. Doorways held open by gravity and habit, with just enough structure to sleep at night when it rained.

People who had every reason to crumble, and still found joy in living.

Michael and I had come to volunteer through Maximo Nivel, an international organization known for its immersive programs that combine language, service work, and cultural exchange, all grounded in meaningful, on-the-ground support.

Antigua unfolded like a living diorama, every cobblestone street and crumbling arch telling its own story. Nothing about it stood at arm's length—it was a baptism by color, sound, and scent. It pulled me in fast; I felt like stepping into a canvas still wet with color.

Time seemed to blur, folding the present into the past. Vibrant paint peeled from crumbling walls, each layer a splash of turquoise, ochre, and coral catching the sun like a precious gemstone. Behind them, thick jungle green curled up the hillsides, and a volcano as alive as the streets.

Tuk-tuks wove through the streets with unapologetic confidence—compact, three-wheeled vehicles. No doors, all nerve. Every one of them came customized: painted windshields, dangling fringe, sun-faded stickers repping soccer teams and saints. Their engines sputtered in uneven bursts, a type of street percussion you felt more than you heard. You didn't sit in a tuk tuk, you got bounced into whatever rhythm the city was already keeping, and honestly, I loved it.

That first evening, Michael and I sat in a courtyard, Gallo con limón sweating against our palms. Fuchsia blossoms from a bougainvillea flower spilled in cascades over sun-worn walls, catching the last of the light. And it was hard not to notice that even the smallest hands were in motion.

Kids barely tall enough to clear a market table weaved between tourists in the courtyard with their arms outstretched

with bracelets, carvings, and paper birds that flipped on cue. Their hands moved fast and sure. Little eyes scanning the crowd, not with wonder, but for opportunity. This wasn't play. It was work.

A boy and girl slipped between tables, no older than six—maybe younger. Siblings probably. Woven baskets slung over their shoulders like they were born carrying them.

The boy stepped forward without hesitation, face smudged with dirt that settled into the creases from a long day. In his hands, he cradled a grasshopper woven from palm leaves; small, intricate, so finely made it looked ready to jump from the tiny hands that had created it.

"Chapulín," he said, presenting it carefully—as if he was handing over something sacred. "Te gusta?" he asked, his voice lifting at the end, just enough to let the hope show.

His sister stepped up beside him, lifting her own creation with the same urgency. "¡Esto es especial para ti!" she said, eyes locked on mine, not playful, to close the deal. Her fingers moved so fast, twisting the palm leaves into a paper doll.

It was equal parts mesmerizing and devastating, how their hands moved with the ease of habit, folding need into something beautiful. They should've been holding crayons, drawing dinosaurs, or running with toys in the square, not hustling for money.

We jumped in fast, one project after another. The first stop was an elder-care home at the far edge of town, in a neighborhood that sagged under its own existence—forgotten, much like the people inside.

The plastic chairs lined the walls, each one filled by

someone waiting, though for what, it wasn't clear. One woman traced circles on her thigh with her index finger again and again, eyes fixed on the floor. A few chairs over, a man sat as still as the paint peeling above his head.

Others sat upright, hands folded, fingers bent and lined from decades of repetition—threading needles, kneading dough, sorting beans, always doing. No one spoke the stories, but they were right there, in the way their bodies had learned to hold still.

Just a quiet loop of waiting.

The courtyard looked like a garage sale had collided with Christmas. Those damn plastic chairs in every color, and a strand of tinsel drooped sadly from a support beam. In the corner, a half-deflated Santa slumped against the wall, looking just about done with it all. It wasn't polished, but none of us were aiming for flawless. The sun showed up, the speakers worked, and finally, the place had a pulse.

The señora in the pink sweater and plaid scarf came in swinging, determined, wobbly, and absolutely ready. The stick trembled in her grip, but her grin said she'd already decided to win. Michael and I tried tightening the blindfold, but she waved us off like we were rookies getting in the way.

Her first swing was nothing but enthusiasm—a huge hopeful arc that sailed a solid three feet wide. The courtyard lost it anyway, cheering like she'd split the piñata clean open. She bent over, laughing from the gut, and the whole place rolled with her. By the second swing, we were part of the riot she started.

Behind us, a few of the elders clapped from their chairs,

their palms landing a half-beat behind the speaker, who was wheezing out "Feliz Navidad." One man leaned so far forward it looked like he was sizing up the piñata for his own turn.

We learned quickly that most people here arrived for one of two reasons: some had simply been left—dropped off like discarded furniture when their care became too hard, too time-consuming. Others came because their families had nothing left to offer, not money, not hours, not energy.

Different stories, same ending: they were brought through the gate without fanfare and guided to a seat in the courtyard, handed a sliver of routine in place of the life they used to have.

Something in their faces made us go quiet, not from pity, but for recognition. Some of these people had built houses, held families together, maybe once danced with someone who made their stomach flutter. Now, they sat beneath sagging banners from holidays long past—plastic chairs, paint flaking from the walls, in a courtyard that had stopped expecting anything to change.

I caught myself watching for too long. Had these older adults once woken before the sun, water boiling, hands already in motion? Maybe they told stories that made the room pause, or laughed so hard they had to lean on the nearest wall. I wondered what their days looked like back when someone counted on them—when they were asked to stay, to help, to tell that story one more time, when their names meant something to someone.

Our next stop brought us to a place called Joy Filled Homes—a name painted tall across the blue cement wall, surrounded by cartoon bees with wide smiles and butterflies in rows. Just beneath it, block letters announced: *Donde niños especiales encuentran su familia,* where special children find their family.

Inside, someone had tried—with every brushstroke—to make joy louder than circumstance. Rainbows arched over green hills and puffy clouds. Painted giraffes and elephants followed a mustard-yellow trail toward a boxy ark, while a red heart curled beneath the words, "Jesús ama a los niños."

I made way for a little girl in a purple sweatshirt wheeling herself to the back, with a teddy bear tucked in her lap like a secret. Out in the courtyard, a playhouse painted in sherbet colors, missing a few shingles, stood slightly off-kilter—mimicking a child's drawing turned real.

Across the green space, clean laundry swayed on the line, casting crooked shadows on the concrete. Barbed wire looped above the walls, crowning the perimeter with steel thorns—watching over a world painted in primary colors and innocence.

The children were as varied as the murals, some bold, some barely audible. One boy gripped the piñata stick like a sword, grinning so hard his eyes vanished into bliss as he swung wide. A girl in a royal-blue sweatshirt lifted a neon tambourine high over her head, her face lit with something bigger than happiness—maybe triumph or freedom in a single moment. Another rocked gently, eyes tracking every movement, saying everything without a word.

She was maybe twelve, and stood out before she even knew I was watching. She wore a bright blue sweater, sleeves pushed to her elbows, the cable-knit stretched slightly at the

shoulders. The girl's hair was parted clean and braided tight, each section clipped with a different color bead—green, red, purple—like punctuation marks in a sentence she hadn't yet spoken.

Her eyes looked at everything without seeming to. Not skittish, not guarded. Just...aware. There was a depth in her stare that didn't match her age.

I asked the program director about her. His stance loosened; the part of him that had given us the tour faded. Then he looked at her, and finally, he spoke.

"Her story is tough," he said.

He told us that she was just a baby. Two, maybe three months old.

When her parents held her the way parents do—with her head tucked close, one hand cradling the back of her neck. No rush, just a quiet walk with their baby in their arms.

Not to visit family. Not to a clinic. And not to a park.

They walked to a dumpster.

One of them lifted the lid. The other leaned in and let her go.

She landed on a bed of wilted lettuce, broken glass, and something sticky that clung to her blanket.

Flies came. Then ants. Then night.

She stayed where they left her, still breathing, cries thinning out between passing traffic and clinking of someone else's trash. By the time someone found her, she'd been lying there for days surrounded by everything the city throws away.

They pulled her from the dumpster; her skin was streaked with grime, her lips dry and cracked. She hadn't been fed in days. Her breath was shallow. Infection had already begun its work.

The doctors didn't sugarcoat it. The damage was done—parts of her brain had gone dormant, and they wouldn't wake up again.

I didn't speak. I just watched her—seeing her small hands wrapped tight around a doll as she smiled, wide and easy—and I couldn't make sense of it.

The world had shown her its worst, and still she looked up and smiled.

Me? I'd been picking at my wound, over and over, nursing pain like it was proof of love. Thoroughly consumed by what had vanished, I forgot to hold what hadn't.

I had twenty-eight years and two days with my mom. Twenty-eight years full of lullabies, birthday candles, and hands that reached back for mine. A childhood where someone always came when I cried. My foundation wasn't perfect, but it held—my mom had always looked me in the eye and stayed even when I didn't make it easy. When I pushed her away. I was never her maybe; I was wanted, and I knew that.

This little girl had none of that.

Her story didn't mean to confront me, but it did. It held something up to my face, and for the first time in a long while, in that mirror I didn't just see damage—I saw possibility.

And in that space, gratitude finally had somewhere to land.

THE NIGHT I DIDN'T DIE

There are moments when the past shows its fingerprints on our lives. Not loudly, just enough for us to see how much of who we've become was shaped before we even noticed.

The clearest example of how this showed up for me happened just a few months after I returned from volunteering in Guatemala.

In 2015, I signed up for another service trip, this time in Ecuador—and on our very first night, the group was scheduled for a guided walk through the Amazon. No flashlights, no path lit for comfort—just the jungle stretching out in every direction, classic immersion stuff.

We left the cabins sometime after midnight—straight into the darkness. The sounds of the rainforest thicken around us. No shoes, because who the hell needs shoes in the Amazon, right?

It was raw. Adventurous. One of those "You had to be there" kind of experiences...

Except—there was no *we*.

It was just me.

Alone. Sleepwalking.

I'd slipped out of my cabin in the middle of the night, door unlocked, steps descended, feet on the ground—and walked straight into the jungle. Barefoot. Asleep. My body moved with purpose while my mind remained nowhere in sight. I was fully committed to a journey I had no memory of choosing.

The next morning, after everyone finished breakfast, Sarah, the program director, caught my eye and motioned for me to come over. She had that careful expression people use when they're trying not to startle you.

"Do you remember anything...different from last night?" she asked.

I laughed, assuming this was small talk.

"Honestly? I'm just nursing a wine hangover," I joked. "But it was a fun night. Ready to get to work."

Her face didn't move. That was the first hint that something was off.

She blinked a few times...then asked me what the last thing I remembered was. "I showered, stretched out on top of the sheets, pulled the mosquito net down, and went to sleep."

"That's it?" she pressed.

"Yeah," I said. But her expression didn't match the simplicity of my answer. Something in her face told me I'd missed a chapter. A faint unease settled in, the kind that

makes you replay your night in fast-forward even though you're sure you didn't do anything worth revisiting.

Finally, I just asked, "Did I do something last night?"

She exhaled slowly. "You really don't remember anything?"

"Sarah," I said, "I swear. I have no idea what you're talking about."

That's when she told me.

"You managed to get out of bed, leave your cabin—didn't wake your roommate. You opened the door, walked down the steps..."

"...and then, for reasons none of us understand, you went to another cabin about sixty feet away. You didn't go to the door, Trey. You went to the window. And you went *through* it. Full body. Straight through the screen and into the room."

She ended the story by explaining that after I crashed through the window, she'd walked me back to my cabin herself.

I didn't try to joke. I didn't try to dismiss it.

"Sarah," I said, rolling up my sleeves, "I have chills. Look at my arm."

I held it out. Scratches ran from my wrist to my elbow, thin lines crossing over deeper marks I hadn't noticed until that moment.

Then I lifted the hem of my shorts.

"And this."

A deep bruise stretched across my side, spreading over my hip and creeping toward my ribs—dark, swollen, impossible to ignore now that I was fully awake.

I told her, "I noticed all this in the shower this morning. Had no idea where it came from. *At least now I know.*"

And the wild part? A piece of me was impressed.

I found the door, the stairs, and even a window—without ever waking up. For someone who needs GPS to escape his own neighborhood, that level of night navigation bordered on supernatural.

But once the humor settled and I actually looked at what happened, the pride evaporated.

I left the cabin after midnight.

In the Amazon.

Barefoot.

Unconscious.

Alone.

The path could've taken me anywhere. Into the trees. Down an unseen drop. Toward wildlife that definitely wasn't waiting to greet me.

I didn't vanish. I didn't end up deeper in the jungle.

Somehow, my body carried me back to a place where someone could find me.

The only way it made sense was that something—God— kept me safe. I shouldn't have walked away from that night with nothing more than scratches and a bruise, yet there I stood. It reminded me of all the other times in my life when I should've fallen harder, when the outcome should've been worse, and somehow I was carried through anyway.

It wasn't an isolated event. There were countless nights when I'd end up out of bed, wandering, or wake up after unleashing a scream that shook the walls. I startled entire houses. I terrified people in hotel rooms. I scared myself, mostly because I never remembered a thing.

I'm not trained in sleep science or trauma psychology, but I know what it feels like to live inside a body that keeps working through the truth you struggle to say out loud. I was processing things at night that I couldn't carry during the day, so they found another exit.

Two years into healing—after real effort, after real change—I still had a reservoir of sadness sitting underneath everything.

You can't destroy it. It just shifts form.

Maybe the goal isn't to wipe the grief out of your life altogether. Maybe the goal is learning to see it differently; to let it teach you instead of haunt you.

THE VULTURE, THE HUMMINGBIRD, AND ME

My sister once shared a metaphor that's stayed with me for years: the vulture and the hummingbird. They cover the same ground. Same sky overhead. Same stretch of earth beneath their wings.

But the vulture's on a mission. It circles with intention, scanning for what's lifeless. And it always finds it. It always uncovers what's decayed, what's been abandoned, what's stopped fighting a long time ago. It never leaves empty-handed because it's trained to look for precisely that.

The hummingbird has an entirely different assignment— less doom scrolling, more treasure hunt. It picks up flashes of color most of us walk past without noticing. It knows where the hidden blooms live, where a bit of sweetness waits in a

place that looks bare from a distance. It finds what's alive, even in spots no one else gives a second glance.

Life doesn't choose one version for us. It delivers both—beautiful moments tucked inside hard ones, joy brushing up against loss, hope sharing space with the mess.

There's always something. The car makes a sound it wasn't making yesterday. A plan falls apart. A chapter closes before you're ready. Some old bruise from your past taps you on the shoulder just to prove it hasn't punched out yet.

And yeah, it spills out sometimes.

You snap at the cashier.

You dodge a call you meant to return.

The vulture in you swoops down and goes after whoever's standing closest.

It happens. It's part of being human.

But walking around like bitterness is a personality trait? That's not deep—it's just exhausting for everyone.

In my last year of college, I was behind the register at the same Borders bookstore I'd eventually be fired from when a woman approached with a single greeting card. No stack of books, no last-minute chocolates—just the card.

I scanned it, slid the card and receipt into the envelope, handed them to her, and gave my standard, "Thanks—have a good one."

She didn't move—just glared at me as if I'd just leaned across the counter, locked eyes, and called her mother a bitch. She stood there holding the card like the transaction wasn't over.

I finally broke the standstill. "Is there something else you needed help with, ma'am?"

She blinked, then tilted her head—insulted to the core. "A bag," she snapped. "I need a bag for this card. I'm standing here...waiting...for you to give me what I asked for."

I pulled my best customer-service smile, reached under the counter, and came up with the largest bag we stocked—big enough for a beach towel or a side table. I offered it to her with both hands, the way you'd hand off a truce.

She let out a scoff. "Don't you have anything smaller?"

"We're out," I said, still smiling. "But hey—have a fantastic day."

Before she could object, I was already waving the next customer forward, both arms out, full runway marshal energy.

She didn't move. Just stood there—broad stance, arms frozen, energy of a bison in the middle of a two-lane road. "Aren't you going to put the card in the bag?"

"No," I said, keeping my smile exactly where it was. "But if the plastic bag feels overwhelming today, I'm confident your large purse can handle it."

"You're a smartass. I need to see your manager."

I did a slow, dramatic turn, paused, and turned back to face her again.

"Hi," I said, locking eyes. "I'm the manager on duty..."

Her jaw tensed. "Unbelievable. Guess they'll let anyone be a manager these days. I'm calling corporate."

"That sounds productive," I said, already reaching for the next customer's item. "Hope your day is as pleasant as you are."

It's been over sixteen years since that incident, and I can still see her standing there.

It was never about me. And it sure as hell wasn't about the bag. She'd been holding something in long before she reached my register, and that moment gave her the opening she'd been waiting for—her vulture finally had something to rip into.

It's a tough pattern to break.

I spent years returning to places inside me that should've been allowed to rest, hovering over old wounds, picking at memories until they were nothing but scraps. I kept going back to my mother's death, father's emotional absence, shame around my sexuality—not to mend any of it, but to confirm the narrative I'd already decided was true about me: flawed, unworthy, too much.

I kept choosing what wore me down simply because it felt familiar. I stayed close to people who left me depleted, repeated habits that boxed me in, and held tight to versions of myself that had expired long before I admitted it.

My humor, my body, my voice, my intelligence, my talent—nothing was safe from my own inspection. I broke myself down in private long before anyone else had the chance, convinced it was better to strike first.

And the whole time, I kept circling my past, convinced it held the only blueprint of who I was allowed to become.

What changed my perspective wasn't that bad magically disappeared—it was that something bright could grow beside it. The vulture in me kept waiting for the world to prove it was as bleak as I believed. But the hummingbird in me started noticing that even in the bleakness, something kept blooming.

My mother's death didn't just mark time; it also rerouted everything that came afterward. I can trace whole parts of myself to that fault line. Before. After. It pushed me forward in ways I never asked for. But in the middle of all that ruin, something steady took shape—an honesty about who I was, and who I wasn't, that I doubt I would've uncovered on my own.

And my father lived on the opposite end of the spectrum. We were polite satellites, passing close enough to acknowledge each other, but never close enough to share the warmth. We weren't going to reenact some sweeping father-son reconciliation from a movie, but he showed up in the ways he knew how.

Growing up closeted taught me more about human behavior than any classroom ever could. It gave me a front-row seat to how people soften when they think no one is watching, and how they harden when they feel exposed. I learned to study those moments, the subtle shifts in expression that revealed the truth beneath whatever story they were trying to project.

Holding my own secret taught me how to move through the world with care. I recognized the flicker in someone's eyes when they were hiding something, and understood that people are layered, complicated, full of contradiction. Carrying my own secret made me gentle with other people's shadows.

It also reshaped my faith. Instead of pushing me away from God, it pulled me closer. And because of that, I don't carry resentment for religious leaders who teach something different. I pray for them—the ones who told kids like me that we were broken or in crisis, when we were simply trying

to understand ourselves. I pray for their healing and ask that the truth remain before them until they choose to see it.

All of it—the loss, the distance, the hiding—left me with a capacity for connection I might never have found otherwise.

The truth is, vultures are not the cause. They're the aftermath—the form we take when gratitude packs up and leaves.

Gratitude is what shuts down the internal alarm system—the one that treats slow walkers, loud chewers, the woman who ignores deplaning orders, or the man unloading an entire week's worth of groceries at self-checkout as some kind of personal attack.

Gratitude walks the same cracked earth, sees the same busted fence posts and sun-bleached bones—but stops for the wildflower clawing its way through gravel. It doesn't deny the wreckage. It just refuses to let the wreckage decide the story.

Just like a hummingbird.

Leading with a thankful heart turns the ego down to a level where people become audible again—where you can actually hear them.

Some days, being a hummingbird is easy—dinner with friends, big laughs, the kind that leave your face sore. Other days, it's a scavenger hunt. But every day, we get to choose what type of person we want to be. And the slightest kindness—the sort you barely register—can be the exact drop of hope someone's been inching toward.

The world isn't going to rearrange itself for us. But the way we look at it—the details we choose to notice, the places we decide to invest our energy in—can alter everything.

CRAYONS AND
CORRUGATED TIN

Traveling brings me joy. Real joy. Drop-me-in-an-airport-with-a-boarding-pass-and-a-latte kind of joy. But for reasons I've stopped questioning, the moment I start packing, that joy short-circuits and turns into a full-blown Olympic event.

I'm not an overpacker—I'm an unapologetic maximalist in a suitcase showdown with physics. Domestic, international, car, ship, plane—it doesn't matter. I pack like I'm heading into exile. My suitcase always ends up looking like it's being punished, zipper barely holding on, contents staged to riot at baggage claim.

And every time, I lie to myself: *This trip, I'll be reasonable—just the essentials.*

Cut to me forty minutes later, cramming in eight

"options" for a three-day trip, because what if I wake up in a different mood? What if the weather shifts mid-trip? What if I suddenly decide I hate everything packed, except for that *one* extra I squeezed in?

But this isn't just about me, my suitcase, or my emotional dependency on "options."

We're all packing, maybe not for a trip, but for life. And whether we realize it or not, most of us are cramming things into our metaphorical suitcases every day. Expectations. Grief. Guilt. Someone else's definition of success. The fear of change. That voice from ten years ago that told you you'd never heal.

And just like my real suitcase, not everything makes it in. There's always that moment when the zipper refuses to budge, and you realize something has to stay behind.

So maybe the real question isn't *what* we pack, but what we insist on hauling with us after the plane touches down.

What beliefs are we still dragging around even though they don't match who we've become?

What old stories are we tucking into the corners of our lives out of habit, not purpose?

And more importantly, what gets pushed out because we're too busy stuffing our bags with things that don't matter anymore?

Sometimes you have to escape your own life just to get a clear look at what's been living in your blind spot. A kid sharing their broken crayon without hesitation. A stranger giving you directions without making you feel lost. Someone sliding over to provide you with space at their table.

Eight years after Guatemala transformed how I saw my life,

I found the same kind of clarity in Dunoon, South Africa. The kids at Harare Kidz College, armed with their mismatched markers and makeshift classrooms, handed me moments that looked simple on the surface, but carried lessons I didn't realize I'd been waiting for.

Dunoon never slowed. The whole place moved on impulse, quick and alert—the ground itself kept everyone on their toes. Kids wove through the maze barefoot, hopping over stones and debris with an ease born of growing up in a world that demands agility. Their laughter carried through the alleys, cutting through the cluster of voices and steady pulse of music drifting from a radio tucked who-knows-where.

Dirt paths twisted through rows of corrugated tin shacks, rust curling at the edges like dried blood. Homes were pieced together with whatever people could find: patchworks of salvaged metal, wood, and plastic tarps—stretched taut like overworked skin. The ones living in old shipping containers stood on higher ground. Those steel boxes didn't need decoration or explanation; their height and clean lines said everything. In a place where most walls moved with the wind, a container meant stability, and everyone knew it.

When I arrived at Harare Kidz College, the noise reached me before anything else—shouts, bursts of laughter, chairs scraping across the tile that stopped short of the walls. The building itself looked like it had been relying on borrowed time, but someone had done everything they could to make the entrance feel bright. Just beside the door, a rainbow arched above the words, "Harare Kidz College."

The front of the school was painted in blues and yellows,

colors that refused to match the wear and tear around them. A hand-painted slogan stretched across the wall: "Feeding Little Minds for a Big Future." Beside it, a cartoon figure with a backpack stood next to a weather chart, each box outlined in careful strokes.

Inside, the kids were packed tightly into narrow rooms. The roof above us was corrugated tin, nailed to exposed beams, and a single bulb swaying overhead like it had been hanging there forever. The walls, though, those walls told a different story. Painted in bold reds, greens, and yellows, they bloomed with hand-cut butterflies and flowers, a different kind of brightness that no lightbulb could offer.

When we opened the box of supplies we brought, every pair of eyes zeroed in on the markers and crayons as if we'd just revealed gold. Hands shot up. Smiles stretched so wide it felt contagious.

We had exactly one speaker, and whatever songs I had downloaded on my Spotify. The plan was simple: turn the classroom into a tiny celebration.

And it happened to be pajama day. Which meant the dancing was mandatory—and already half as much fun before the music even started.

The first note of "Flux" by Bloc Party, an indie rock band, hit the speakers and leapt across the room before anyone had time to brace for it. Bloc Party didn't ease into anything—*Flux* came in hot, a rush of sound that electrified every corner of the room.

The reaction was instant.

Tiny feet hit the tile like it owed them money.

Pajamas blurred into wild streaks of motion, dinosaurs, teddy bears, cartoon stars dancing like their lives depended on it. Faces lit, cheeks rounded with laughter; they weren't performing for anyone. They were simply alive with the music, moving with the kind of freedom adults spend decades trying to relearn.

"Flux" made perfect sense. The wild edges of the song matched the way this place breathed—nothing polished, nothing staged, just life spilling out in every direction. Before the beat hit, it was already theirs.

The afternoon before our project wrapped, I stood just outside Harare Kidz College with the principal, sunlight catching the painted metal siding and the cartoon characters along the wall—bright reminders of how far this place stretched beyond its physical footprint.

Up close, her expression told more than her voice ever needed to. There was a calm to her face, but not the fragile kind people use to mask worry. Hers came from years of being the person everyone else looked to when something went sideways. She carried that responsibility in the way she planted her feet, in the way her shoulder stayed set, in the way she watched the courtyard—constantly scanning, always protecting, even while talking to me.

Without raising her voice, she tipped her chin toward the two-story building across the street. "Do you see that building?" she asked.

I nodded.

Across from us stood a skeleton of cinder blocks, stacked in uneven rows. Some had been patched; others left rough, the

seams filled with a mixture that looked as if it had been scraped together from whatever materials were available that day.

Its lower level had two windows trimmed in white paint, long since surrendered to dust. Above it, the second floor waited—open rectangles where windows should have been, the interior exposed to the sky.

The sun hit the corrugated tin nearby and bounced off with no mercy, turning the metal into a mirror that forced you to squint before you could process the rest of it. The whole scene looked paused mid-sentence, as if construction had been interrupted by life itself and never allowed to resume.

She nodded toward the building again, then spoke with a sort of restraint that comes from holding a story in your throat for far too long.

"Four units. No insulation. Barely any ventilation," she said.

The layout came into focus as she described it—each floor cut into two narrow sections, the rooms stacked tight on top of one another. She didn't rush through the numbers.

"Eight people in one space," she added. "Sometimes more."

The math didn't need emphasis—four small rooms. More than thirty people pressed into a structure that looked unsure of itself.

She held my gaze for a moment, then asked, "How many people do you think died in there from COVID-19?"

It wasn't a rhetorical question. It was placed directly in my hands, and she waited long enough for it to settle. I didn't answer. I wasn't really sure how to.

"None," she said.

"Not one."

I blinked. "Like, zero?" I asked, as if I'd misheard her.

She gave me a single nod, then continued:

"People in that house did get COVID. But they recovered. In that sense, they were fortunate." She paused, letting the distinction settle. "And yes, the virus took lives here—neighbors, families close to us. But that wasn't the part that broke us."

"You've seen how we live," she said, her eyes moving from the school to the rows behind it. "This is what we have—and we're grateful for it. But life in Dunoon was already difficult long before the pandemic. The virus didn't begin our problems. It pushed what was already fragile past its limit."

She adjusted her robe at the collar, then continued, not pleading—simply honest.

"I'm able to keep this school running because of programs like SAVE...the one that brought you and your family here. Support comes from people in the U.S., Canada, Europe, and Australia. We don't receive steady funding for schools or communities like yours.

"That's why outside support isn't a bonus for us," she said. "It keeps this place alive."

Her voice choked mid-sentence. "Our community matters," she said, her eyes tracing the street as if she could see every family who'd passed through it. "South Africa pulls people in. From Mozambique, Namibia, Botswana, Zimbabwe...they come because they believe there's a chance for more here. A chance for their children. Many of them end up in Dunoon."

She let that sit for a moment before continuing.

"These children—my pupils—went more than two years without anything steady," she said. I had to close the school. The government required it. And lockdown here wasn't what you experienced back home." She shook her head once, slow, deliberate. "We couldn't work. We couldn't step out. Everything stopped in Dunoon. Completely."

"One of the only ways we understood what was going on was through the Internet from Elon Musk's Starlink," she said. "We're so grateful to him for that."

She didn't linger on it. Instead, she pivoted to what came next—what she did when the classrooms fell silent. She described turning the school into a soup kitchen, stirring pot after pot until supplies thinned. When the soup was gone, they stretched bags of rice as far as they could. And when the rice finally disappeared, she went days without a meal.

"And still," she said devastatingly, "that wasn't the worst of it."

"Many of these children come from abusive homes... during lockdown, no one could step out. Everything stayed inside with them. The fights. The drugs. The assaults. The rapes." She said each word plainly, without softening or dressing it up. "Children were trapped in rooms where there was nowhere to run, packed into spaces already stretched past breaking."

She looked toward the building across the street again, then added, "Babies were born in the middle of all of that. More mouths to feed. No increase in food. No relief."

Then let out a slow breath, not dramatic, just tired.

"No one reported any of it. No cameras. No Stories. No

one came. We lived it every day, and the world moved on like we weren't here at all."

"What COVID-19 did to my community…" She paused, searching for the right shape of the truth. "It left trauma everywhere. The lockdowns broke us."

A tear slipped down from her cheek, and she brushed it away with the back of her hand—quickly, almost habitually, something she'd been practicing through years of holding everything together.

"Even when other countries started opening, South Africa stayed closed," she said. "For a long time. You're the first Americans I've seen in more than two years."

She stepped forward and pulled me into a hug. When she thanked me for the week with her students, it wasn't to be polite—it was real, spoken from a place that had gone without encouragement for too long.

"Volunteers give me hope," she said softly. "For the first time in years, I can see a break in all of this. I can see the possibility again."

I understood why the kids ran to her the way they did. She was the anchor in place where one was needed. Not loud. Just unmistakably present. Her words stayed with me long after she stopped speaking—settling in slowly, like a bruise you don't notice until someone touches it.

The building looked the same when I walked away, but it didn't greet me the same way. The chipped cement, the rust along the tin panels, the weary lines where the structure tried to stay upright—none of it read as construction flaws anymore. It read as proof.

I could see the stories pressed into those walls. If you stood there long enough, you could almost sense what they'd absorbed: cries no one answered, the slap of rage, the silence of a child who'd learned survival through stillness.

There were no plaques. No reports. Nothing to mark what happened there. It was a monument to what people lived through when no one was watching.

That's why the dance party mattered. It wasn't noise or distraction. It was resistance. Proof that something bright was still alive in them.

On our last day, I found myself watching the kids in a new way. Maybe it was everything the principal had shared, or it was the way they moved through the courtyard with no sense of how much had been asked of them.

As they jumped and spun and laughed, one thought kept circling my mind:

They shouldn't still have this spark.

Not after lockdowns.

Not after the empty kitchens and the fear no one names.

And yet—they glowed anyway.

That's what I saw, not broken kids.

They moved as if joy wasn't optional, like humming-birds do.

We decide on what we think we need to pack and carry through life—stuffing every fear, every insecurity, every version of ourselves into emotional luggage that could never fit in an overhead bin.

But those kids, and the principal, showed up with the emotional equivalent of carry-on bags. Not because they lacked depth, but because they didn't hide what was inside. Nothing zipped tight. Nothing disguised. They moved with what they had, in plain sight.

So while my suitcase on the flight home was still one zipper-pull away from exploding. Somehow, I came back carrying less. Because when a kid with nothing hands you a broken crayon and still dances like the world hasn't let him down, when in fact, it did. It made me ask myself something I wasn't ready for:

What if they're the ones who have it right?

SPREADING THE LIGHT

It matters when someone looks at you and doesn't just recognize your presence, but recognizes you. Not in the loud gestures people love to post about, but in the exchanges most never see. The stranger who holds a door open a few extra seconds. The friend in a room who uses your name in a room where you feel invisible. A message that shows up on your phone out of nowhere—no agenda, just, "Thought of you."

Those moments travel through people in ways we rarely acknowledge. You can't trace the path of it, but you can feel the ripple it creates as it moves from one person to the next. For years, I believed that kind of light belonged only to certain people. But the older I get, the more I realize how wrong I was. Light isn't a personality trait. It's the simple practice of noticing. It's the choice to see what most people move past.

Light lives in that kind of consistency, in the small, deliberate ways someone reminds another human being, "You matter, and I noticed."

I think about that little girl in Guatemala more often than anyone would guess. She smiled at me like she carried the sun inside her, as if to say, *This is what I have to give.*

And it was enough. Her light reminded me that even when you feel like you have nothing, there's always something you can give. That even in the dark, there's still beauty. Kindness remains.

The more you give it away, the brighter it becomes.

But light isn't only found in moments that feel warm or easy. Sometimes it shows up through loss, the kind you fought against with every bit of strength you had. There's a particular clarity that hits when something you begged to keep slips from your grip. You watch it break down piece by piece until all that's left is the truth you couldn't see before: what it really was, not the version you spent years trying to believe in.

In my life, everything had to come apart before anything honest could begin. None of it was graceful; it was a full-scale teardown.

If you're imagining something poetic, don't.

This wasn't a phoenix rising.

It was closer to a drunk uncle stumbling through a family gathering, tripping over the buffet table on his way out, leaving everyone frozen in disbelief, while you pretend you didn't invite him.

Uncomfortable as it was, that demolition cleared space for a life that could finally breathe.

Choosing to look for what's good and spreading light doesn't erase the past. Staying open, leaning toward what feels true, none of that sends the dark parts packing. Grief doesn't clock out. Trauma doesn't disappear because you've decided to live with it differently.

It hangs out in the back, popping up in weird places—some stranger's weirdly specific perfume that pulls you back twenty years without warning. A line in a movie blindsides you, and suddenly you're sitting with a version of yourself you thought you'd outgrown.

The difference now is that I don't set a place for it. I don't hold open the door, offer it a drink, and let it settle in. When those echoes rise, I acknowledge them, and then I keep moving.

Eleven years after my mom died, I was chasing a certification to teach group fitness for about a million reasons. Working remotely, my days are a loop of Teams messages and video calls. As an extrovert with the social battery of a golden retriever, I needed real people in front of me, breathing the same air, and reacting in real time. Every time I pushed through a workout, the clarity was unmistakable, almost medicinal, and the idea of sharing that feeling with others felt right.

Then came the practical steps between me and the instructor's headset. And there it was, sitting at the bottom:

CPR certification.

Before I could even think about verification, the app walked me through a short video on how to use my phone as a compression guide. The idea was simple: set your phone on a couch cushion—anything with a bit of give, start the program, and let the sensors judge your technique.

Straightforward. In theory.

I followed the instructions exactly—cushion on the bedroom floor. Phone balanced in the center. I was kneeling beside it like I was about to propose. I hit *start* and got to work.

Almost immediately, the timing was off by just enough to annoy the app, and it made sure I knew it. Each alert... heckling me. Full-blown "Boo, you suck," energy from a piece of glass and aluminum.

Not enough pressure.

Too slow.

Incorrect tempo.

By round three, the app had gone full mean-girl. Every beep had the vibe of a board judge at a talent show, tapping her pen and whispering to the other judges, *"Is this really what we're working with?"*

So there I was, on my bedroom floor getting roasted by an algorithm while punching a cushion—just trying to pass a CPR module before my next client call.

In my frustration, the room faded away,

One second, I was kneeling on my bedroom floor, wrestling with a couch cushion and an app that clearly hated me. Next, I was somewhere else entirely. Leesburg. The rug under my knees. My phone pressed to my ear. The dispatcher's voice cut through a wall of panic.

And my mom, motionless in front of me.

I hit a breaking point. A full-body collapse onto the rug, mid-workday, next to a couch cushion that had absolutely

seen enough. I was crying so hard I could barely breathe, nose running—the whole tragic mess.

And through it all, the CPR app kept chiming in, offering feedback no one asked for.

Somewhere in all of that, I realized I had less than eight minutes to get my life together. Eight minutes to stop crying, rinse my face, and somehow morph back into a functional adult before a brand-new client logged into a video call.

Nothing screams "you can trust me with your business" like showing up freshly destroyed, eyes still glossy, hair giving off post-storm vibes.

I stared at myself in the camera preview, trying to decide if I looked more like a haunted Victorian child or someone with a serious illness.

When the client logged on, I smiled like I hadn't just been ugly-crying into my carpet. She was in Virginia, working for a major financial institution based in North Carolina, and we eased into the conversation with the usual warm-up questions. I always try to start that way—human first, business second.

We traded small talk. Music came up, and she lit up, telling me she was a diehard Hootie & the Blowfish fan. She lost it when I mentioned that my best friend's husband actually knows Darius Rucker—they go all the way back to high school. Whatever composure she'd been holding onto just evaporated. She leaned back, laughing, hand over her mouth, like I'd revealed a state secret.

Then she got quiet, the joy still lingering in her expression but fading at the edges.

"I needed that," she said. "Something good. It's been

a tough year." She hesitated, steadied her voice, "The first anniversary of my dad's passing was last week. It's still hard to say out loud."

The second the words left her mouth, she blinked like she hadn't meant to let them escape.

"Sorry," she said quickly. "I know that's not exactly professional...I don't know why I said that."

Given the emotional CPR rehearsal I'd had on my floor twenty minutes earlier, the timing felt too pointed to dismiss. It made me look up—like God had pulled up a chair and tapped me on the shoulder. Not subtle. Not a coincidence.

So I told her.

Not everything. I didn't unravel the whole history or hand her every detail.

Just the outline: my mom passed. It happened quickly. It changed me in ways I never expected. I'd stood in the same kind of grief she was describing. I knew the language it spoke, even when you don't want to hear it.

"Thank you," she said, almost a whisper.

She exhaled, an extended, shaky release she'd probably been holding for weeks. "God, I feel ridiculous—we don't even know each other."

"You don't need a deep personal relationship," I told her.

Once you've lived through it, you start to recognize the frequency. Maybe she was meant to hear it from someone who could answer in its native tongue. Just to remind her: *you're not alone.*

You don't need a title, or a platform, or even a close relationship to make an impact. Most of the time, you don't

even know when you're doing it. Light slips through the cracks anyway.

A little girl in Guatemala.

A principal in South Africa.

My mom, who taught me more about love and fight than she ever understood she was teaching.

Each of them handed me something I still carry. And maybe that's what spreading light really is, not saving the world, just illuminating your corner of it.

Because you're carrying something someone else needs.

All you have to do is stay open long enough to notice it.

THE SPACE BETWEEN
US ISN'T THAT WIDE

By now, it's probably obvious I'm no stranger to questionable decisions. I've marched myself into situations I had absolutely no business being in—armed with a level of confidence that should've required a permit.

We've all been there.

Reacting when you meant to pause. Saying something that sounded wise in your head but came out sounding more like a pure asshole. Snapshots that didn't reflect who you are at your core—just who you were in that particular, emotionally-charged, possibly sleep-deprived, frayed-at-the-edges moment.

Because being human isn't easy, and none of us gets it right every time.

There's no shortage of voices telling us who we're supposed

to fear. Social feeds, talking heads, headlines built for outrage—an entire ecosystem working around the clock to convince us that we have nothing in common.

Little by little, they wear us down.

Not all at once, just enough that we start sorting people into boxes instead of looking at their faces. Just enough that disagreement feels risky, like saying the wrong thing might cost us connection rather than build it.

We forget there's an actual person on the other end of the screen—someone with history, a heartbeat, someone whose absence would ruin somebody's day, someone loved by at least one human being in this world.

But you can't find clarity in a room that only echoes you back to yourself.

And you can't offer understanding to someone you've stopped seeing as a person.

The truth is far simpler than everything we use to complicate it.

Your zip code, your bank account, the shade of your skin, the name you whisper in prayer, the person you fall asleep loving, the little box you mark on a ballot—none of it steps in when life decides to drop you to your knees. None of it blocks the blow.

We're all going to hope for something better.

We're all going to laugh until our ribs ache.

We're all going to dance at least once without worrying who's looking.

And one day, every single one of us is going to leave this place behind.

Strip away the labels we grip so tightly—the titles, the categories, the arguments, the armor, and what's left is the level where we meet each other.

That's where we're the same.

When I started performing stand-up, I learned something that rewired the way I saw people: nothing pulls strangers into the same room faster than the truth you didn't plan to admit. No setup can compete with that.

We assume humor lives in the punchline. It doesn't.

It lives in the unscripted—the line that slips out before you've had a chance to pretty it up. And the more profound the truth behind it, the harder the room responds. Not because the joke is flawless, but because the honesty connects first.

But in real life, we don't volunteer everything we hide in plain sight:

The insecurity that lingers right behind the compliment,

The relationship hurdles we tiptoe around,

The job that looks great on paper but leaves us strangely empty,

The pressure to keep it all together because everyone assumes we already are.

You probably don't bring it up.

Most of us don't.

But whatever your "it" is, somebody out there drags around a version of it that feels close enough to be a twin.

If you've ever shared something honest—sincere—you already know what happens. People don't connect because you're flawless or fascinating. They connect because the honesty underneath it lets them recognize themselves.

We aren't drawn to each other's polish.
We gravitate toward the cracks we were told to repair.
That's where people feel less alone.
That's where the distance between us closes.

EVERYTHING I BURIED GLOWS

You don't wake up thinking, *I'm grieving* or *I'm damaged*. You wake up wondering why your phone alarm sounds like it's trying to start a fight. You tell yourself you're tired, behind, just need one solid weekend away for catching up—even though "caught up" hasn't been your reality in years. Maybe you're dehydrated. Maybe you need magnesium. Maybe it's everything hitting all at once.

So you snap. At your partner. Your kid. A stranger who double-parked as if they were making a personal statement about your worth as a human being. And later, you're staring at your phone, typing into ChatGPT: "How do I stop acting like a dick to everyone?"

And honestly? It makes sense. You've been carrying too much for too long—but who picked this oversized plate in

the first place? Who keeps piling more on it as if you signed up for some endurance challenge no one warned you about?

Why me?

Why this?

Why won't anything change?

You circle the same questions, calling it reflection, but really you're just pacing the perimeter of your pain—examining it from every angle, waiting for it to collapse on its own.

How much time have you spent tending to the remains of a story that ended years ago? How much of your time has been lost on something that stopped serving you long before you realized it?

So picture this...

You're sitting under harsh fluorescent lights that make everything feel colder than it is. A paper gown sticks to your back, thin as tissue and twice as useless...trying to breathe in a room that smells like antiseptic and old conversations no one wanted to have.

The doctor walks in.

She's holding a folder with your name printed neatly in the top corner. Then she opens the folder and proceeds to read from a single sheet of paper:

Two words at the top, bolded like they're shouting.

Stage Four.

And in that instant, everything you swore mattered—your to-do list, your inbox, the fight you had yesterday, the false narrative replaying in your head—falls straight through the floor.

Your mind doesn't jump to the comeback you thought you'd make, or the promotion you were chasing, or the last thing you bought that felt important for five minutes. All of that evaporates. What rises instead are the questions that suddenly dwarf everything else:

How much time do I have left with the people I love?

How much life have I postponed because I assumed I had endless tomorrows?

The future stops feeling like a guarantee and starts looking like a privilege you never realized you were counting on. Certainty was never the baseline. It's an oversized blazer slipping off our shoulders, sleeves swallowing our hands like kids playing CEO.

Every one of us is a second away from our lives looking nothing like they did five minutes earlier.

Life doesn't wait politely in the lobby.

It doesn't ping our calendar before the biopsy results drop.

We don't get a vote on timing the big stuff.

We only ever get *now*.

And strangely, that's where the miracle is hiding—because even without control, we still get to decide what our damage becomes.

We love to imagine change as some cinematic finale—spotlight overhead, music swelling, and a neatly worded monologue that ties things together so it all makes sense.

But that rarely happens. It slips in through small pivots.

In the half-second pause, we decide to breathe instead of letting autopilot run the show. When we interrupt your usual

lineup of go-to reactions, or avoid firing off a surprisingly hostile three-word response to an email.

We choose not to be the older version of ourselves.

We choose, instead, to offer grace.

Not because it's been earned—grace isn't a reward—but because we remember what it felt like to stand at our lowest, hoping anyone could still see something good in us.

And then, we do it again.

And again.

Those tiny mercies stack. They start to change the way we move through the world. Our eyes catch what's bright, constant, and life-giving before they fixate on what's falling apart. We move with a lighter curiosity, drawn toward what's alive instead of camping out in what's already decayed. They reintroduce us to the parts of our lives still reaching for us.

Then one day, almost by accident, we look up—and realize we're no longer standing in the same dismal place we started in. We stopped treating our damage like a crime scene and started treating it like a source.

That's when we'll start noticing what survived.

What stayed, including the damage we buried.

It's been lighting your path underneath the entire time.

Every heartbreak.

Every loss.

Every version of us that crawled through a year we thought would take us down—each one left something behind and pushed our roots deeper into places no one expected life to spring from.

We didn't become who we are by accident. Our lives

weren't forged in the absence of damage, but through it. So perhaps the damage wasn't the villain we made it out to be, but rather the first sign we were waking up.

And maybe that's the part we miss while we're too busy sprinting away from our own lives: the very damage we thought would mark us forever is the same damage that taught us how to see clearly, and to recognize the choice to live with intention.

Damage loses its power when we stop treating it as something that happened to us and start living with it as something we can use—a point of reinvention, and a decision to rebuild.

EPILOGUE

Almost ten years passed before I could look back—at *everything*—without bracing for impact. When I finally sat down to write, the parts of me I'd spent years avoiding stepped forward without hesitation. They filled the page with everything I'd tried to outrun: the losses, the failures, the guilt, the nights that felt endless. But they also brought back what I'd neglected to honor: the grit, the humor, the small signals of hope that kept breaking through, even when I couldn't see them.

Somewhere in the middle of all that, I understood why I was writing at all. It wasn't to rehash the damage, but to turn it into something useful, something that might help someone else feel less alone inside their own version of it.

The first draft came faster than I expected, in April 2023, a few weeks after the ten-year mark of my mom's death. The year that followed was spent shaping it into something I could hand to a publisher without breaking into a cold sweat.

By early 2025, I'd signed with Ripples Media and stepped into the editing process, where you spend a million hours across the table from versions of yourself you once tried to leave behind. Every chapter felt like pulling out a chair for another former self and letting them speak.

Somewhere in that stretch, I rewrote the final chapter. In it, I had imagined a scene I'd never lived: a doctor seated across from you, offering a diagnosis that bends your reality in one direction with two words and a look that confirms everything before a syllable leaves their mouth.

Stage Four.

Really uplifting content, I know.

The scene was meant to show how quickly life can reorganize itself. One moment, your mind is juggling errands, deadlines, and the constant swirl of a thousand small obligations. Then something hits the room with such clarity that everything else falls away.

For months, that moment only lived on the page—a controlled environment, safely contained and purely hypothetical.

Then July arrived, and that imaginary room stopped being imaginary—the line between what I'd written and what I was living dissolved in an instant.

That year was designed to shine.

Michael and I were marking twelve years together; he was stepping into fifty, and I was rounding the corner toward forty. Our circle of friends had their own milestones cued up,

and we also had job promotions, a publishing deal, one kid heading into senior year, and another just starting high school. For a moment, it felt like every door in our lives had decided to open at once. We kept joking about collecting milestones in bulk, stocking the shelves full before life remembered it had a different itinerary.

In January, Michael traveled to Germany. February placed me in the Dominican Republic, celebrating my best friend Jessica's fortieth with sun, drinks, and an unreasonable amount of inside jokes. By March, I decided to get a jump start on my birthday and booked seats in Atlanta close enough to the stage that I could see the sweat fly during the Deftones concert with Michael.

That night, over dinner before the concert, I kept giving him a hard time.

"I'll have tap water—ice cold, please," he told the server.

I looked at him. "Tap water? Ice cold? Who even *are* you?"

Michael, who'd happily drink molten rock before touching an iced beverage, was now asking for still water chilled to extremes—an abrupt departure from his sparkling-only identity. It had been going on for about a month. He nudged his food around, taking small bites without interest. He'd even ordered a beer, lifted it for one sip, tried again out of obligation, then set it aside like it belonged to someone else.

So I did what any supportive partner would do: I drank it.

This was coming from a guy who normally treated menus like adventure manuals—a total foodie, the one who'd choose the strangest entrée just so he could tell the story later. But little by little, he started pushing away the foods he loved most. First salmon. Then red meat. Then all meat. Then coffee joined the list.

"Maybe you're pregnant," I said, laughing, reaching for humor the way I always do.

One more departure from his usual self, Michael had always been the one reaching for an extra blanket while I slept one degree shy of spontaneous combustion, fan blasting through every season. Then, almost overnight, the man who treated seventy-nine degrees like winter—Mr. "Can we turn the heat up?" became Mr. "Why is it hot in here?" He'd kick the blankets aside and start fanning himself, running warm in a way that used to be exclusively my domain.

But the exhaustion cleared any chance of a joke. Michael had always been up before the sun, coffee ready, gliding through the first hours of the day with a drive that made everyone else look unmotivated by comparison.

So watching him drag himself out of bed felt wrong. He'd stand there, hands on his knees—hyping himself up just to start the day. And once he did, he moved through the hours with the caution of someone rationing energy he wasn't sure he still had.

When Michael came home, he'd sink into the couch— eyes without their usual spark, shoulders slumped. He looked less like someone finishing work from a job he loves and more like someone returning from battle.

Between May and June, he met with two different doctors, and both closed the appointment with reassurance that felt prepackaged. Stress, they said. One floated "hormones" as a possibility, but in the way you mention a distant relative, you

don't actually expect to show up. They ordered a handful of basic labs—check-the-box panels—and every result slid back across the portal, stamped "normal."

There were no follow-up questions. No curiosity. No map of next steps. Just a polite nudge toward the exit and a suggestion that whatever this was would simply fade on its own.

"Try limiting screen time before bed," one of them offered, as if blue light were the culprit.

I'm not a clinician, but you don't spend two decades in and out of hospitals with your mom—learning to read her face, her breathing, fluctuating stability—without developing a sense for when something deeper is at play.

By late June, the stairs became Michael's Everest. Halfway up, he'd stop, both hands pressed to the wall, trying to steady himself. This was a man who'd always moved through the world with ease, now skipping meals, barely sleeping, and struggling with mobility. No version of that pointed to screen time.

At the start of July, he met with a functional medicine doctor, and for the first time in months, it felt like someone was actually paying attention. New labs were ordered. They ruled out Lyme, ruled out mono, it wasn't mold, and noted his testosterone was running a little low, but nothing that matched what we were seeing at home. A full allergy panel followed, with messages ping-ponging back and forth as results trickled in. It wasn't a diagnosis, not yet, but we were moving toward something instead of pacing the same circle.

Her examination raised the possibility of fluid in his abdomen, so she scheduled an ultrasound for July 24th.

That afternoon, I was easing out of a client lunch, weaving through the parking lot, when Michael's name lit up my phone. His scan had only been a few hours earlier.

I answered, expecting a quick update.

Instead, he spoke with a controlled calm I knew too well—the kind a person uses when they're trying not to hand this fear to someone else.

"The doctor called," he said. "She sounded upset."

That word—*upset*—stuck in my throat. "Upset?" I asked, replaying every appointment from the past few months, every time we were there, it was nothing.

He took a breath before continuing.

"Yeah. She said the scan showed what looked like hundreds of tiny lesions on my liver and was concerned it could be cancer. She's already setting up an appointment with an oncologist, and they want a biopsy."

For a minute, I couldn't tell whether I was in that parking lot or inside the last chapter of my book. Nobody expects to hear those four words together from a doctor...*they're concerned it's cancer.*

In that instant, life stalled. I was going through the motions, but everything had a faint delay, as if the world were buffering. By the time August 8 arrived, the date of Michael's liver biopsy, it felt like we'd already lived the moment repeatedly, running every possibility throughout our minds until the days blurred together.

Nineteen days. Four hundred fifty-six hours. Two random Tuesdays between the first time we heard the word *cancer* and the day everything split into *before* and *after*:

The third Tuesday arrived—August 12.

The scene felt eerily close to the one I'd written months earlier. Michael and I sat beneath fluorescent glare, waiting for the oncologist. The light washed the room of depth—walls, chairs, the plant in the corner, even us reduced to outlines. He sat to my left, shoulders pulled in, his shirt stretched across his distended stomach. The fluid built up fast, and now it looked like he was carrying a full-term pregnancy.

I'd been in rooms like this before, rooms where time thinned, where you sat suspended between the life you'd lived and the one you might be walking into.

A pair of knocks broke through the stillness, and the doctor stepped inside. Laptop in hand, eyes fixed on the screen first, then on us.

I stood automatically, unsure of why. Habit maybe. The reflex to appear composed, like posture, could control the outcome.

She pulled the stool toward us, the wheels squeaking across the tile, and settled in with a breath that delivered the truth before she even spoke a word. We both felt the direction this was heading, but it still existed in the distance, something happening to someone else, somewhere else.

"Your initial liver biopsy results came back," she stated, voice measured, careful. Too careful.

She looked at Michael first, then at me, as if dividing the heaviness of the news evenly between us. "From the tissue sample collected at the biopsy," she continued, "we can confirm that you have cancer. Adenocarcinoma—cancer of gland-forming cells."

Her words arrived in fragments, syllables that took their time before making sense. *You have cancer.* That phrase felt like a door quietly closing somewhere behind us. At that moment, cancer stopped belonging to pamphlets or statistics. It attached itself to our lives, immediately and permanently, and the world we knew ended at the period of her sentence.

There was no outburst. No gasp. Just a stillness that said, *I already knew, but I was hoping you'd tell me I was wrong.*

The doctor kept going, outlining steps and referrals in a rapid sequence that read more like a battle plan than a medical update. My hand cramped before I'd finished writing the first sentence, the pen pressed so hard into the page it nearly stopped writing. I pushed through it, forcing the ink across the page, sure that if I could capture every detail, the situation might feel more manageable.

"We'll need several more tests to pinpoint where the cancer started," she said, her eyes moving between us. "One is an immunostain panel. It helps trace the cells back to their source—lung, stomach, pancreatic, or bile duct." She paused long enough for the possibilities to settle, then continued. "Alongside that, we'll run a molecular profiling test, a PET scan, a CT scan, and Caris testing. Those will show any mutations and guide us toward treatment options."

"The fluid in Michael's abdomen is from the cancer," she said. "We'll arrange a paracentesis to drain it. That should ease his breathing and help him sit comfortably."

She explained her theory next. The liver didn't appear to be the starting point. The biopsy from the week before suggested it was a secondary site, evidence of spread, not

origin. Michael's AFP levels, a marker that usually climbs in primary liver cancers, were relatively low. It pointed to a tumor growing elsewhere in the digestive tract, which then moved through the body before settling in the liver.

I wrote everything down without fully understanding what it meant. All I knew was that we hadn't found where it started, that it had already spread, and that hearing it laid out so plainly made everything clearer—and harder to take in at the same time.

In that exam room, as the diagnosis took shape, we came face-to-face with the heart of *Good Damage.*

ACKNOWLEDGEMENTS

Without God, none of this exists.

To my mom, for never quitting on me, even when I gave you reason to. I think about you daily. I recognize you in my total lack of direction, in the way laughter takes over my whole body, and every time I'm tempted to believe something can't be done. I watched you do what others said couldn't be done, again and again. That example lives in me.

Michael, I said I was writing a book. You replied, without blinking, "Picture book?" Your sense of humor is *almost* as good as mine. Thank you for supporting me every step of the way on this journey. You opened the door to something I never thought I could have, and I love you and the kids so much.

My sister, Tobilyn. You stepped in where our parents couldn't. Your grace, wisdom, and faith steadied me during years that felt overwhelming and unstable. You showed up consistently, and that mattered more than you'll ever know.

Jess, We've always recognized each other. You're an unstoppable force, and without your friendship, your influence, and your belief in me, I wouldn't be where I am today.

Connor, Kayla, JP & Toler. Watching you grow up is the best thing I get to be part of. I love you.

Sallye, I'm grateful to have you in my life through Michael. Thank you for all your encouragement to write this book!

Andy Suggs, your friendship and creative mind (visually) brought *Good Damage* to life. I'm forever grateful.

This book was in process for decades; I just didn't realize it at the time. I can't move forward without first taking a step back to 2013: Mo, I wish I knew your last name. Thank you for sitting with me in the worst moment of my life - without hesitation. Nicole Davis Wilson, you were my rock in Leesburg. Shrop, even with distance, you're still family, you drove 130 MPH to get to me when mom passed. Thank you.

Thank you, Jessica + Adam Zapia + Brown Family, for making me part of your family the first Thanksgiving after mom passed. Forkel + Family for opening up your home to me for the first Christmas without my mom.

Dinah, you and your family embraced Michael and me with open arms—thank you.

Thank you to everyone who reached out, prayed for Michael, checked in on us...and extended grace during my long stretches of silence in 2025: Jen + Ryan Bass, Dia, Jess + Mark, Amanda White, Grant + Flo, Diane Brasher, Danny V. + Miriam, Lauren & Greg Goad, Mike & Magda, Dana + Jody, Thomas + Meredith, Mary Osorio, Blake McClean, Amy & Josh Blum, Angela Myers Miles, Sharron Harris, Tameka Fooks, Ramesh Sundarham, Kiran Bhandari, Greg Bishop, Tatiana Zuniga, James Whitaker, Jeannine Occhipinti, Liz Levy Ward, Tachelle Anderson, Erin Edmondson, Wonya Lucas, Scott Christopher, Maureen Kelly, Joe and Kathy Sindorf, OTF Crew: Anja, Karen, Chris, Danielle Horne,

Cristell Whitfield, Maggie, Seth Klebe + Ansley, everyone at Christ the King for the daily prayers, the 11Alive team, infinite daily support: Melanie Williams, Christine Lyle, Kate Gilman, Casey Broday and Morgan Allen. Abie Peacock, Lori Reeves, Nancy + Larry Lemer—and many more.

Forever grateful to Atlanta Cancer Care: Dr. McKee, Joy, the exceptional care team: Jenine, Shelley, and Charlene. Biggest thank you to Dr. Bindiya Gandhi, MD...you saved Michael's life.

Thank you to the artists whose influence runs through these pages and my life:

Margaret Cho.

Deftones' release of *Private Music* got me through the tail end of one of the hardest years of my life and the final push to write *Good Damage*. Thank you for being the soundtrack of my life.

Lacey Sturm + Flyleaf: for a long time, your music was the closest I could get to God, and it kept me there. Lacey, *Kenotic Metanoia* was on repeat while I wrote. Thank you for that.

Alanis Morissette, growing up closeted in the South during the '90s, was the ultimate mental marathon. Your music gave me somewhere honest to go when I couldn't be. Thank you.

Blindside, I found your music as a teenager and stayed with it. "Withering" and "Painting" specifically helped me reset when my own thoughts weren't getting me there.

Ripples Media:

Andrew, thank you for believing in this project and in me, long before we formally partnered. That early confidence mattered.

Nicole, I'm deeply grateful for the time and patience you gave and sitting in the weeds with me, working through dozens of subtitle options until it was right.

DMF, without you...none of this runs the way it should!

Jeff Hillmire, thank you for your vision and for building Ripples Media into the positive energy machine that it is.

Joe and Kathy Sindorf, you operate as a true team. Your guidance, creative partnership, and belief shaped *Good Damage* in ways that simply wouldn't exist without you. You showed up fully for this work, and I'm deeply grateful.

Lastly, if you read *Good Damage*—even just part of it, I'm grateful.

I want to hear from you.

If anything in this book stuck with you—underline it, screenshot it, whatever—I want to hear from you! Find me online and send me the line that stayed with you, or tell me what you're walking away with.

IG + TikTok: @Toler_the_Trey
Substack: @TreyToler1

ABOUT THE AUTHOR

Trey Toler writes with the velocity of someone used to keeping a room engaged and the sensitivity of someone who learned early how to read what isn't being said. Raised in the American South by a single mother with chronic illness, he stepped into adult awareness young and never fully stepped back out of it.

He writes from a life spent adapting—first to illness and early responsibility, then to loss, identity, and the aftermath of both. His background in stand-up comedy shows in his ability to sit with devastation and still make room for humor. Trey's writing earns its laughs through observation and carries its emotional charge through raw, unfiltered storytelling,

allowing laughter and grief to coexist on the page—the way they do in real life

Years after losing his footing, Trey noticed a pattern: people trusted him with the parts of their lives they hadn't figured out yet. *Good Damage* grew out of those conversations—written to take what helped in those rooms and make it available to anyone who needed that same sense of company. He believes the impact doesn't decide the story—what people choose to give their attention to afterward does.

Professionally, he works in business development with a foundation in marketing and community-building. He previously served as President of Fuse, Atlanta's member-based marketing and advertising organization, where he shaped the environments that helped senior leaders, business owners, and emerging talent find one another. Trey is also a comedian, speaker and moderator, hosting rigorous conversations on professional development, perspective, and the discipline of intentional growth.

Alongside his professional work, he's involved in global volunteer initiatives, leadership development, and advisory roles focused on helping people move with more clarity and less noise.

Trey lives in Atlanta with his partner, Michael, is a stepfather to his children, and shares the house with Ted, their unfairly handsome English cream golden retriever.